W9-AIV-361

FRENCH GASTRONOMY

ARTS AND TRADITIONS OF THE TABLE

ARTS AND TRADITIONS OF THE TABLE

Perspectives on Culinary History

Albert Sonnenfeld, series editor

Salt: Grain of Life, Pierre Laszlo

TRANSLATED BY MARY BETH MADER

Culture of the Fork: A Brief History of Food in Europe, Giovanni Rebora

TRANSLATED BY ALBERT SONNENFELD

French Gastronomy

The History and Geography of a Passion

Jean-Robert Pitte

TRANSLATED BY JODY GLADDING

COLUMBIA UNIVERSITY PRESS

New York

Columbia University Press wishes to express its appreciation for assistance given by the government of France through the Ministère de la Culture in the preparation of this translation.

COLUMBIA UNIVERSITY PRESS
Publishers Since 1893
New York Chichester, West Sussex

Library of Congress Cataloging-in-Publication Data
Pitte, Jean-Robert, 1949–
[Gastronomie française. English]
French gastronomy : the history and geography of a passion /
Jean-Robert Pitte ; translated by Jody Gladding.
p. cm. — (Arts and traditions of the table)
Includes index.
ISBN 0–231–12416–3 (cloth)
1. Gastronomy—History. 2. Cookery, French.
I. Gladding, Jody, 1955– . II. Title. III. Series.
TX637 .P57 2002
641.'01'3094—dc21 2001028637

Columbia University Press books are printed
on permanent and durable acid-free paper.

Printed in the United States of America
Designed by Linda Secondari
Spot illustrations by Martha Lewis

c 10 9 8 7 6 5 4 3 2 1

The sky was blue, all smiled, I left the table, I was happy.

—Gustave Flaubert, *Voyages*, VOL. I

The trip was a delight. The blue mountain, in the warm mist, seemed far away. . . . The stubble fields of the villages streamed with light and celebration, even the trees' shadow was completely permeated with light . . . and Dodin, pointing to a hare that was flying between the muddy feet of a cow, in front of the tottering gray stones of a little vineyard wall:

—What wonderful country! Look, Rabaz, what a powerful combination: the animal, the cream, the wine . . . an entire stew!

—Marcel Rouff, *La Vie et la passion de Dodin-Bouffant*

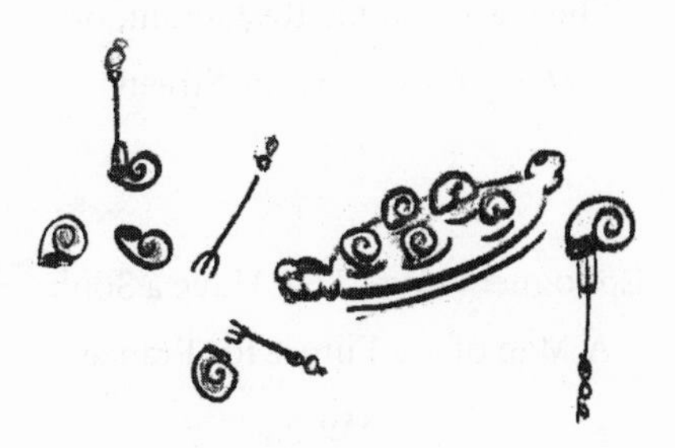

CONTENTS

FOREWORD

FOR GENERATIONS OF ENGLISH SPEAKERS, *gourmand* and *gourmet* were wicked French words, and no post-Cromwellian Anglo-Saxon has ever found an equivalent expression for "bon appétit."

Thus, French language hegemony: our prominent food magazines today include *Saveur*, *Bon Appétit*, and *Gourmet*. The inaugural (January 1941) issue of the latter featured columns entitled "Bouquet de France," "Gastronomie sans Argent," and "Spécialités de la Maison," as well as a culinary lingo quiz asking for definitions of *bisque*, *sauté*, *ragoût*, *petits fours*, and *à la* just about anything, enough to send us all posthaste to sign up for a Linguaphone course!

Jean-Robert Pitte's splendid and entertaining analysis of the *History and Geography of a Passion* offers the most original, complete, and eminently readable explanation of, and justification for, France's most enduring empire: gastronomy. Now we can understand why the French, in the words of Gertrude Stein, "not only talk about food but talk about talking about food."

Pitte, professor of geography at the University of Paris-Sorbonne, is in many ways the creator of the field of "cultural geography," or space as culture. To be understood, a place must be personalized. Landscape is created by mankind as a "culture." The ecobalance of open-space farming and forest land, a gentle humanized contrast to the cruelly deforested American plains, didn't just happen spontaneously; it was a response to the Gallo-Roman hunger for a balanced diet (meat brought in by the hunter and produce grown by the farmer). This balance was made possible in turn by the low population density that has always characterized France, perhaps a result of the French clergy's more relaxed ecclesiastical attitude toward sexuality.

To be sure, as a geographer, Pitte takes account of the usual truisms about France's moderate yet diverse meteorology. France has some six hundred regions or microclimates, which allow Mediterranean, Atlantic, and Alpine agriculture to flourish. Then there are the rivers that, unlike those in Italy, never dry up, ensuring provisions of freshwater fish to complement the saltwater catch from coastal regions. The great gastronomic centers of Paris and Lyon grew up because of river systems leading from the surrounding farmlands directly to the markets: the Seine flows from east to west, the Rhône from north to south. Other culinary capitals (Bordeaux, Marseilles) became such thanks to their maritime harbors.

But *cultural* geography is truly interdisciplinary, incorporating ethnography, ecology, chemistry, biology, meteorology, and the study of the senses. For example, there are "smellscapes." Certain regions, or even small and sharply delineated urban neighborhoods, may have characteristic odors. What is the linkage of those smells to the climate, soil, commerce; to the population's culinary habits; and to occupations practiced?

An especially useful adjunct to cultural geography is history. So I know the reader will find the chapter "Is Gourmandism a Sin in France?" to be particularly enlightening and as "delighting" as I did. Here, one can revisit the wonderful film, *Babette's Feast*. In contrasting the attitudes toward food of French Huguenots and Catholics, Pitte demonstrates that unlike the austere tradition typified by the precepts of the Calvinist Jean-Jacques Rousseau, the French Catholic ethic was anything but ascetic, rather a good-natured conception of the sins of sensuality. Cardinal de Bernis only celebrated mass with a fine Meursault, "so as not to make the Lord grimace at communion time." Nothing is too good for God.

The religious associations of the word *passion* imply suffering resulting from high or excessive commitment. The French national passion for gastronomy, *au contraire*, is, while perhaps obsessive, painless and pleasurable. "Happy as God in France" was a German simile much paraded about earlier in the twentieth century.

In preparing this short foreword, I had thought to skim the pages of Pitte's book. Though I had already read it thoroughly at least three times, I found myself rereading and savoring every word. I know the same happy learning experience awaits readers of this edition.

Albert Sonnenfeld

PREFACE

The *Kugelhopf* Mold

IN 1871, MARIE-MADELEINE WENDLING, born scarcely seventeen years earlier to a family of Alsatian peasants in Grüssenheim, near Colmar, came to Paris, determined to remain French. In her meager bundle, an unusual object commanded a special place: a *Kugelhopf* mold (she pronounced the word "kouklouf" with an accent she never lost). The object dated from the marriage of her mother, Catherine—that is, from 1840. This humble utensil, seemingly flimsy judging by what it was made of but rendered indestructible by its sentimental value, never ceased to be useful. It was for this, to some small extent, and for a few other symbols, that Alsace and Lorraine became French again. A million dead to recover the territory that served to fashion a cake mold—that's a lot. But the soul of beloved objects has no price. That was what Marie-Madeleine thought watching Henri, her son-in-law, set off with a flower in his gun, and the entire bright young future with him, from the East Station where she had arrived in Paris the century before.

Henri died in Verdun, and Marie-Madeleine became the head of the family of her daughter, Alice. Almost despite itself, the *Kugelhopf* mold took the place of the lost one, and each holiday, Marie-Madeleine poured a batter into it that she mixed and beat with such prodigious passion she could raise and lower the receptacle's central axis in her enveloping affection. Then she carried it, wrapped in her shawl, to the baker's oven. Jeanette, her granddaughter, stared wide-eyed at each of these mystical celebrations. She inherited the mold and the magic know-how after Marie-Madeleine, and then Alice, died.

As if so much care had turned it into bronze, the *Kugelhopf* mold is still alive and, with unabashed success, regularly bakes the cake that Catherine prepared 150 years ago. Its marbled patina glows with the thousand fires of butter mounds that have polished it and held in the depths of its valleys the split almonds cooked in their skins.

Our family mold is a gentleman, to whom this book owes much, just as it does to Marie-Madeleine, my great-grandmother, who was able to pass on to her descendants a fondness for eating well.

This work does not claim to review in detail the whole history of eating, cooking, and table manners in France. Excellent individual syntheses exist, as well as many scholarly works, which have been used here. It focuses on gastronomy, whether everyday or extraordinary, modest or extravagant, and considers it from the perspective of geography, that is, from its allocation in space. Rather than examining the star-studded map of regional cuisines and great restaurants, it attempts to answer a question that involves the whole country and its inhabitants: Why are the French—or why do they believe themselves to be—the enlightened eaters, the gourmets?

Last year, while working on a survey on French taste today, I met with Michel Guérard and asked him that question. "It's genetic . . . ," he responded immediately. I made a face. Two days later, I received a telephone call from him. "Excuse me, I answered your question too hastily. In the end, it cannot be genetic; only education can explain the phenomenon."

Of course! The French are not born with it, have not acquired this body of knowledge or taste in a day, and are not the greatest gastronomes for eternity. If they want to maintain this particular aspect of their culture, of which they are so proud, they have to struggle daily, each time they go to market and each time they sit down at the table. To have high standards for the food on one's plate is also to have high standards for the whole farm-produce chain and oneself. To remain an oasis of optimism and *joie de vivre* in the French imagination, to avoid becoming a vague memory of times gone by, the garden of delights requires jealous care and vigilance at every moment. To understand its genesis can help us gain awareness of it.

Villars-Fontaine, December 1990

Marie-Madeleine's Recipe for KUGELHOPF

This cake, its recipe dating back to the middle of the nineteenth century, is very different from brioche; it has none of that airy softness. Traditionally, it is a basic peasant loaf for Sunday breakfast and holiday dessert. It has a good crust and solid middle that doesn't evaporate the moment you move your tongue. Alas, it is impossible to find anything like this today in Alsatian bakeries, where *Kugelhopf* is nothing more than vapid brioche with raisins and almonds, sometimes dominated, *horresco referens*, by the taste of orange-blossom water. . . .

INGREDIENTS

500 g (3 ¼ cups) flour
2 eggs
100 g (⅜ cup) sugar
250 g (9 oz., about 2 sticks) butter
20 g baker's yeast (about ⅗ oz. or
1 cake compressed yeast)
a pinch of salt
half a bowl of Malaga raisins
whole almonds with their skins

PREPARATION: In an earthenware bowl, vigorously mix the flour, eggs, 200 g (7 oz.) melted butter, sugar, salt, and yeast dissolved in a little warm water. Then add the raisins. Grease the inside of the mold with the remaining butter and stick the almonds to the hollows in the sides. Pour in the dough. Let it rise in a warm spot (a 30°C [85°F] oven) for several hours. Bake at medium heat (350–375°F) for 30 minutes until the loaf has covered the hub in the center of the mold. Take out of the mold when cool. *Kugelhopf* is wonderful for breakfast, but also for a snack or dessert, washed down with a Gewurztraminer or an old Tokay.

LIST OF MAPS

FRENCH GASTRONOMY

Introduction: On France's Gastronomic Passion

Of all the European countries, France is by far the one that grants the most importance to its gastronomy, and for many generations, the French have shared the almost absolute conviction that the world's best cooking takes place on their soil. A magazine published recently by the French Alliance of Mexico states, "Of all European peoples, only the French are truly interested in what they eat. . . . This we can be sure of: when a restaurant in the Western world is famous for its cooking, it is the tricolor flag that hangs above its stove. And when, in Munich, Zurich, or London, someone happens to demonstrate above average cooking talents, he has learned everything from the French."[1] This is far from an isolated example of such crowing. As an IFOP/Gault-Millau poll revealed in 1977,[2] 84 percent of the French population considers French cooking to be the best in the world; only 4 percent give preference to Chinese, and 2 percent to Italian or North African.

This fact is nothing new. As early as 1884, Philéas Gilbert constructed the great imperialist dream of creating a school devoted to universal gastronomic synthesis,[3] where "it would be possible to do a geography course . . . in which each country would appear with its food products. . . . Alimentary riches from the entire world would flow to the school, which, in turn, would distribute them, marked by that stamp of genius our culinary luminaries know how to impress upon whatever leaves their hands, to the great good fortune of our modern gourmets."

In imagining a National School of Culinary Arts—the stillborn project of Ecully[4]—Jean Ferniot took up Philéas Gilbert's ideas in his report on the promotion of the culinary arts, presented to the Ministers of Culture and Agriculture in 1985.[5] There he wrote in all seriousness, "Cooking is a French art. . . . If French cooking has attained perfection, it owes this, of course, to its creators, but also to its products. . . . One has never eaten and drunk so well as in France today. . . . Perhaps France is still alone in being capable of training chefs, while others train cooks."

But the French would be subject to ridicule if they were the only ones to believe they were the best. The great art lies in having been able to convince all of Europe and the developed world of this without ever demonstrating any real superiority. Only the Japanese resist that subtle machinery of persuasion in considering our great cuisine to be skillful and sensual, but theirs to be more philosophical, poetic, and healthy.[6] The Chinese, for whom gastronomy rose unscathed from the ashes of the Cultural Revolution,[7] remember that with regard to food, if not cooking, their own sensibility and that of the French maintain an odd complicity.[8] As for declared enemies, there are hardly any left on the horizon. The Anglo-Saxons take delight in our escargots and our frogs, and Nemeitz's recriminations from the early eighteenth century are no more than a bad memory now.[9] "Nearly everyone believes," he wrote, "that you eat well in France, and especially in Paris, but they are mistaken; that is for certain." Moreover, the bitter traveler immediately qualified his remarks: "Those who have the means and people of quality eat well, retaining their own cooks, because French cooks have the edge over all others, whether it is a matter of invention, or the selection of meats." That remains somewhat true for this late twentieth century, insofar as there is a difference between the sad, poorly defrosted stews served in many cafés and the fine food of creative restaurants.

Expressions of respect and allegiance flow from all parts. Like those of Queen Victoria in the last century,[10] the banquet menus for the White House are written in French, "the international language of gastronomy," as the press service points out.[11] This is a vestige of the time when French was also the language of diplomacy and culture. The short story by the Danish author, Karen Blixen, *Babette's Feast*,[12] recently adapted for film, constitutes a lovely Scandinavian tribute.

Among the thousand other testimonies: the preface of a very widely distributed Hungarian cookbook reads,[13] "From the beginning, our best restaurant owners and our most skillful chefs have had the ambition of assimilating everything the art of French cooking has produced, in order to be able to offer it to their guests." In 1985, in the Paris metro, advertising posters paid for by the Italian Exterior Commerce Department vaunted its country's food products. An appetizing strip of ham from San Daniele was seen elegantly wrapped around a fork with this text addressed to the French: *the best cooking in the world loves distinguished guests*. Israel, Hungary, and other countries produce excellent foie gras, but the psychological climate is such that it would be unthinkable for this liver not to be processed in Périgord, where it must go to be anointed by France (this phenomenon cannot help but remind us of French fashion and perfumes).

Such a convergence of praise, added to the general French interest in the pleasures of the table, poses a real historical and geographical question. When and how did French high cuisine originate and flourish? Why in France and not in Italy or some other European country, since—do we need to repeat it?—choice dishes and food lovers exist throughout? England, which has such a bad reputation on this side of the English Channel, possesses its fair share of fools for unusual gustatory sensations. What about those "happy few" from the Savoy for whom that great London hotel charters a helicopter so they can sample Scottish grouse as early as August 12—"The Glorious Twelfth," the opening day of hunting season for this celebrated fowl?[14] Nor must we forget that without those food lovers across the Channel, there would be no Bordeaux, no port, no sherry, no Madeira, etc.[15]

Whatever the reality about French excellence, it is important to understand the process that allowed that reputation to be established, but it is just as important to ask what it is that distinguishes eating well or gastronomy from the everyday diet. The boundary, no doubt, is difficult to draw with precision, and especially with objectivity. "Only a man of the mind knows how to eat," wrote Brillat-Savarin, because he digests both food and the fantasies his mind has secreted. Under those conditions, a slice of real bread, a spoonful of Cotentin soup fat, or a shirred egg can be just as gastronomic as ortolans or red currant jam seeded with a goose feather as they know how to do in Bar-le-Duc. Among other things, it was by the way they prepared a shirred egg—this simple dish requiring, besides a very good egg, a very sure stroke—that Fernand Point used to judge the cooks who sought employment with him.[16] Gastronomy, like a passion for music, is a form of aestheticism acquired by constant, intensive cultivation of the senses, the most important, in this case, being taste.

For the average person, the sense of taste is long left lying fallow and widely cultivated short of its potential during big dinners and occasional banquets over the course of which, through lack of good judgment, quantity and pretense prevail over quality. For the gastronome (who, to achieve the heights of pleasure, sometimes sinks to pathological fussiness, so common among aesthetes), every food, every drink is a pretext for emotional fireworks. For the uninitiated, the most sublime dish is only a scandalous waste, or, in the best cases, simply food, more or less agreeable. The geographer Paul Clavel tells how, as a child in Quercy in winter, he was nauseated by the scent of the truffle ragoûts his companions brought in as they reheated all morning in lunch pails on the stove of the school where his mother taught. Thus, neither he nor those who consumed these particular ragoûts felt the delicious thrill Satan inspired in the celebrant of the *Trois Messes basses* by putting into his head the thought of "two magnificent turkeys, stuffed, stretched taut, marbled with truffles."[17]

Fortunately, fanatical perversion or *gastronomania*, which excludes all abandon and all humor, is rare in France. It survives among certain professionals, critics, cooks, and members of clubs. Grimod de La Reynière sometimes falls into it; like Lucullus, he does not consider it beneath him to eat sumptuously . . . alone, which is another form of perversion. The

French readily share the feeling that eating well is too agreeable to be neglected, but also too agreeable to be taken too seriously, exaggerated academicism and absence of lightness spoiling part of its essence. Berchoux, Brillat-Savarin, or, more recently, James de Coquet illustrate this tendency and this deadpan tone. The origin of the word "gastronomy" itself does as well; it is actually very French, beneath its Hellenic exterior.

Popularized in 1801 by Joseph Berchoux in a long poem of more than a thousand alexandrines,[18] republished six times between 1803 and 1829 and translated into English and Spanish, it corresponds to that form of humor—French, but more especially English—which consists of using a pseudo-scholarly word or a neologism to designate an everyday reality. "*Gastronomie*" is a transposition into French of the title of the lost work of Archestrate, the grandson of Pericles and great lover of unusual and varied gustatory sensations, its existence known to us only through the quotes in Athenaeus's *Deipnosophistai*. The word had been used for the first time in a translation of that work in 1623[19] but had not then escaped the bounds of erudition. To name the thing it would henceforth designate, the word "*gourmandise*" (gluttony) was used, having lost its sinful implications to become merely offensive; or "*bonne chère*" (eating well), that is, "good cheer," which fortunately remains in use; or again "*friandise*" (delicacy), which had become slightly outdated before being reduced to the simple rank of "*sucrerie*" (sweets). Overly pompous and slightly blasphemous, "*gastrolastrie*" (the religion of those devoted to Gaster, "stomach" in Greek), which we owe to Rabelais's imagination,[20] never really took hold. Like "*gastronome*," "*gourmet*" also connotes the informed consumer, that is, one who takes an interest in what he eats and drinks, judging the quality of everything.

The whole history of *haute cuisine* is summarized in this long progression from "*gastrolastrie*" to "*gastronomie*" and the international acceptance of the latter. "*Gastrolastrie*" was a literary attempt at ennobling voraciousness and piggishness. What the word depicted had become more and more the prerogative of the working classes. Also, slang, very rich in these matters, proved more apt than scholarly language in responding to the needs of enthusiasts for such excesses. There are at least 104 words or expressions, most of them crude, that the French use to talk about eating in excess.[21]

Two centuries after Rabelais, piggishness has become the utmost vulgarity for the cultivated elite. The word "gastronomy" lends a scientific and professional air. The "legislation of the stomach"—since this is the literal meaning of a word well suited for attracting the pen of a man of the law like Berchoux—testifies to the fact that refined eating is no longer reserved for the high born, but open to all who enjoy a little wealth, leisure, and sense of pleasure. The word ratifies the union between intellectual culture and eating well. It improves upon a sensual drive, transforming it for good into art.

This refinement in cooking and eating accompanied the whole cultural development of the elite, whereas elsewhere in Europe it remained more or less behind for various reasons, allowing for the success of French cooking outside of France. Louis XIV already dined on delicate and complex dishes while Madame Palatine, his sister-in-law, was still relishing robust sauerkraut drenched in beer. For those who recognize the gulf between true sauerkraut and its sad substitute, there is no doubt that this peasant dish can be a matter of gastronomy, but the Sun King had not learned to exercise his subtle gustatory skills on that type of cooking. As we will see, had he taken pleasure in it, sauerkraut would undoubtedly have joined the battalion of *haute cuisine* recipes.

Without claiming to precisely define the rules of gastronomy, we can nevertheless acknowledge that it calls upon the sense of taste, of course, but also upon the other four senses, which is not the case with any other artistic expression generally classified as such. The beauty of forms and colors (the dishes as well as the table and the decor); the aromas; the sounds of precious liquids flowing, flaky pastry, and crisp grilled meats; the feel of crystal, silverware, and fine table linens, the slippery, resilient, or crunchy consistencies of the dishes: all converge to create a harmonious atmosphere recognized by the guests and part of the conversation, the sign of a special moment.

The success of a gastronomic moment owes as much to the appeal of sensations already familiar and known by heart as to the effect of surprise, novelty, exoticism in the raw materials, how they are used, and the surroundings. Now this effect can be obtained just as well by creating complex compositions as by exploiting a coarse, wild flavor with exceptional evocative powers the cook must know how to retain. For the gastronome, stimulated by one place and one time period, the right taste is a sensation sought at each meal and requiring sensitive nerves, taste buds, and cultivation on maximum alert. And as is the case in the plastic, musical, or literary arts, the more he practices, the more difficult it becomes for him to achieve complete satisfaction. He who takes delight today will be disappointed tomorrow if he doesn't reach a higher degree of refinement. Even being deprived of food can be an excellent stimulant for the imagination, as the all-beef meal Marshal Richelieu served to notable prisoners proves, as does the New Year's feast served to those lodged at the zoo during the siege of Paris in 1870.

Nor can we forget that gastronomy has always maintained complex relations with dietetics. These two sets of precepts constantly evolve in space and time and are very sensitive to fashions, which does not help them achieve harmony. Sometimes they are very much in opposition, sometimes they converge, and they are always keeping a watchful eye on each other. The human organism expresses essential needs but also proves itself to be very flexible. Certain products presented to it for the first time correspond immediately to its needs and thus enter into its range of preferences. Others, on the contrary, are rejected for either or both physiological and cultural reasons, and thus will never become gastronomic. Still others attain recognition—from the stomach and the mind—after a more or less lengthy purgatory. The French gastronome achieves a subtle mix of solidly grounded traditionalism and active curiosity. We find this state of mind in Alexandre Dumas,[22] for example, but also in many of today's "*nouveaux cuisiniers*," and thus in their clientele. Most of the great works in the history of French cooking couch their recipes in peremptory dietetic principles, and this is true from antiquity up to Michel Guérard's *La Grande Cuisine minceur.*[23] The funny thing is that those principles are constantly changing!

Gastronomy also maintains close ties with the landscape and the social environment. There are some gustatory sensations forever inscribed in gold in the memory or giving rise to literature. Some dishes usually considered ordinary can become sublime in certain circumstances and surroundings: the smoked herring sandwich devoured in hearty bites and washed down with aligoté in the morning freshness of a Burgundy grape harvest, the roasted chestnuts on a Paris street corner on days of icy fog, the fried mussels enjoyed on Ostende or Knokke-le-Zoute's wide beaches are as much gastronomic pleasures as Trois Empereurs foie gras savored on the seventh floor of La Tour d'Argent overlooking the Seine. Salvador Dali perfectly conveys the intensity of this feeling in his *Dîners de Gala*. The description of the meal at Dumaine at Saulieu[24] reveals the exceptional gastronomic sensitivity of the Cadaqués master:

> One evening at Saulieu, M. Dumaine said to me, "See that veil of mist, halfway up the poplar hedge. Above the foliage, the sky is clear, the stars are out. At the foot of the trees, you could count the truffles. Prepare yourself, it's on such evenings, when the fog floats at this exact height, that I can succeed at the *pâté en croûte* I am going to make for you." I sat down at the table, contemplating the countryside, and my gastronomic pleasure was extreme. That same pâté, without this speech, I had gulped down distractedly. I have to be told that a dish is exceptional for my taste buds to quiver.

One more testimony to pay homage to the late Alain Chapel, that "cathedral" of contemporary *haute cuisine*, as one critic graciously called him:

> It is just as important, for the cook as for his guests, to try to reunite in the plain chant of delight the taste of the *omble-chevalier*, the Lake Annecy landscape, and, for example, whatever quartet Fauré wrote not far from what would become Father Bise's Auberge.[25]

No doubt many Europeans and inhabitants all over the planet are capable of such thrills—Dali was Catalan—but perhaps there is a higher than average proportion of French who seek them out and carefully cultivate them. It is that geographic peculiarity of the Hexagon we will attempt to understand here. In this way, we will also make Michel Onfray happy, whose opinion is unfair but serves our present purposes:[26] "Only a gourmand's geography is not boring."

Chapter One

France: The Land of Milk and Honey or the Old Country of Gourmands?

French Cuisine and Wines—The Myth of Canaan

When wine growers, oenologists, scientists, or simple wine lovers try to understand why France produces good wines, they often look toward the soil or the sky. In the 1960s, preparing a thesis on the vineyards of the Burgundian coast, Rolande Gadille traveled the *grands climats* (in Burgundy, "*climat*" refers to the soils and the wine they produce) of the Gold Coast to collect the thermometers she had installed there and to measure the albedo index (the percentage of luminous radiation reflected by a given surface), very high, for example on the calcareous clays where the Corton-Charlemagne Chardonnay ripens. She concluded that, "The more or less perfect harmony between microclimatic and geopedological action alone can account for the degree of success attained in wine production, conveyed by the personality of the *cru*."[1] And we can still picture the sadly missed Bordelais geographer, Henri Enjalbert, and his disciple, René Pijassou, walking over the Médoc gravel fields, weighing the stones in their hands, assessing their proportion in the soil, verifying how their roundness allows for good drainage, and thus demonstrating the superiority of the *grand cru* soils, the prize going to Château Latour.

Nor can the role of weather be denied in the success of a vintage. Bernard Hudelot, a rogue wine grower and oenologist of Nuits's high coasts, maintained with good reason that the vintage of 1989, a year of anticyclonic stability and a particularly warm autumn, would surely never attain the heights of 1988, favored by those important diurnal variations that made the vines "suffer" and solicited from the pinot vine stock its very best. We also know how the daily transition from warm mist to dryness is essential in the Sauternes region for the harmonious development of *Botrytis cinerea*, responsible for noble rot and the great vintages.

Thus, a temperate climate manifesting all its variations, good exposure, good drainage, and the right granulometric and chemical composition of many soils is enough to account for the huge number of good and very good French wines. But then how to explain that one can drink bad or mediocre Chambertin, and that certain soils in Berry, Poitou, or the Haute-Saône plateaus produce no wine even though they are rich in potential? Moreover, don't the great wines come from soils rich in potential, certainly, but also from acrobatic feats of adaptation by viticulturists at the cost of constant effort? Witness, for example, those eighteenth-century drains in the trunks of hollow pines found buried in the ground in a few great Médocan domains.[2] In certain operations, doesn't the use of gas heat or mist sprayers (the mist freezes and protects the sprouting buds) now allow for production of champagne or Chablis year round? Finally, you have to drink the wine that the late André Noblet—the great master of Burgundian wine and spirits who officiated for more than forty years over the Romanée-Conti domain—produced for his own use from the mediocre, clayey soils of the Vosne plain to comprehend how care and know-how are easily as important as the soil.

As Roger Dion said, "The role of the soil in the development of a *grand cru* scarcely exceeds . . . that of the material in the creation of a work of art."[3] The essential thing is knowing how to make the material speak! No *David* of Florence without the fine Carraran marble, but nothing, first of all, without Michelangelo and nothing, either, without Medician patronage. No d'Yquem without the raised mounds of well-drained gravel, but nothing either without the expertise of the landowning families, the present one, the Lur-Saluces, having pursued the policy of quality since 1885 and skillfully maintained an extraordinary reputation. Nothing either without a international clientele ready to pay the price of gold for each bottle bearing this signature.

In a country like France, the soils that allow for creating a noble product are legion. Through the course of the Middle Ages and the modern period, viticulturists have known how to recognize a certain number of them and exploit or improve them as necessity required. And the only necessity, becoming a law, has always been and still is that of consumption. Roger Dion demonstrated this in a striking way by unearthing and commenting on these superb words of Olivier de Serres, written in 1601: "If there is no place to sell your wine, what will you make of a great vineyard?"[4] That being the case, is it at all surprising that today's great wines, nearly all of them heirs to ancient reputations, are, as a result of the policy of the INAO (*Institut national des appellations d'origine*), situated in immediate proximity to a market traditionally demanding luxury products or a trade route allowing access to one?

Would the wine of Champagne have seen the light of day

without the counts and the fairs that made its reputation in its red version in the Middle Ages, and then without Saint-Evremond, who made the English come to appreciate it in its "white sparkling" version, and then without the Regent, and then without the court of Louis XV, who made it the symbol of celebration and levity in high Parisian society?

Would the burgundies enjoy such prestige if the coast they came from were not situated close to the ancient capital for the dukes and a major travel route for medieval Europe, leading both to the Parisian basin and toward the northern plains? Would the Cîteaux monks, vowed to asceticism, have perfected the viticulture of their Vougeot vineyard to such an extent if they hadn't received all Europe's mighty and powerful at their abbey?

Would the wines of Sancerre, Bourgueil, Chinon, and Anjou have developed if their lands hadn't bordered the Loire navigation route, if Paris hadn't been so close, and if the kings hadn't made the Loire Valley "France's garden," showcase for their courts' and their own prestigious residences?

Of course, Châteauneuf has at its disposal pebbly terraces that make the vines "suffer" and require of them the effort giving rise to the *grand cru*, but would this latter have seen the light of day if the City of the Popes and their courts hadn't been so close? As Alphonse Daudet so pleasantly describes it in *La Mule du pape*:

> Every Sunday, leaving vespers, the dignified man [the pope] went to pay courtship [to his vineyard]; and when he was up there, sitting in the good sunshine, his mule beside him, his cardinals all around him spread out at the feet of the root stocks, then he had a bottle opened, a *cru*, that beautiful ruby-colored wine which was then named *Château-Neuf-des-Papes*.[5]

As for Bordeaux, its wines would be mediocre without the English market for which they were specifically developed as early as the Middle Ages and without the great eighteenth- and nineteenth-century families of magistrates, merchants, and bankers who were destined to make Chartrons the greatest international port for exporting good wines to England, northern Europe, and the United States. When, like Lafite, you have clients as prestigious as Jefferson, president of the United States after being its ambassador to France, you spare no expense, thus, through reduced yield and perfected technique, allowing only the best to be produced. Still today, no Médoc château hesitates to downgrade a wine that could tarnish its reputation. In the last century, seven years have been too mediocre for the Lur-Saluces to produce d'Yquem (this is also the current attitude of the great houses in Champagne, which only produce their premier vintage wines in good years).

Conversely, since the Middle Ages, what could have prompted Parisian viticulturists to produce good wine, since it was so easy to sell new Suresnes wine to the people of Paris, who probably did not have the means, moreover, to buy any other brew? As for the capital's powerful and mighty, supply was assured by the area upriver from the Seine or the shores of the Loire.

The same logic applies to all the large metropolises: Lyons and its Beaujolais, Nantes and its Muscadet or its Gros Plant, Bordeaux and its Rive Droit or its Entre-Deux-Mers. With the industrial revolution and the railroad, which lowered the cost of transport, Languedoc was able to launch itself headlong into quantity and mediocrity, in order to quench the thirst of northern France's working-class throngs.[6]

What is true of vineyards and wine is just as true of cooking, and it is a serious mistake to believe France to be a country where milk and honey flow spontaneously, where you only need to bend down to gather the most exquisite manna fallen from the sky. In his memoirs, Auguste Escoffier, who dominated Western *haute cuisine* a century ago, holds such a position:

> I am often asked for reasons why French cooks are superior to those of other countries. The answer, it seems to me, is simple: you only have to realize that French soil has the privilege of producing, naturally and in abundance, the best vegetables, the best fruits, and the best wines in the world. France also possesses the finest poultry, the most tender meat, the most delicate and varied game. Its sea coasts provide it with the most beautiful fish and crustaceans. Thus, it is completely natural for the French to become both gourmands and great cooks.[7]

Nevertheless, the flaw in this deterministic profession of faith appears in the two sentences immediately following the cited passage:

> But in order for a nation to have good cooking, it must have a long history of courtly life leading to the appreciation of celebrating a good meal with friends, just as it must have solid domestic traditions passing on from mother to daughter all the secrets of a fine table. In the renown of our French cuisine, I would hope to see proof of our civilization.

That being the case, why not just admit that high-quality produce is as much the work of humans as of nature, that without gastronomes there would be no talented cooks; no producers of good vegetables, good fruits, good wines, good poultry, good meats; no hunters skillful at managing the cynegetic inheritance; no fishermen capable of flushing out the best fish and seafood; and that, when all is said and done, it is not so "natural" that the French become gourmets and that they succeed in satisfying their appetites?

Of course, France is not any less favored than other countries. There is no denying that its position at the heart of temperate Europe offers it a great variety of agricultural possibilities. But after all, isn't that also true for Italy, the Iberian Peninsula, the Balkans, and, in a general manner, almost all of Europe? Moreover, haven't fine cuisines developed in small regions or even in cities: Périgord, Bresse, Alsace, Tuscany, Bologna, Lyons, Fès, Kyoto, or Canton? All this reduces to nothing the standard argument revolving around diversified environments.[8] Insofar as we can speak of "regional cuisines"—and we will come back to this idea—it is certain that they are not more varied in France than elsewhere in the world. But here again, we are dealing with one of the most familiar clichés, accepted as much by the French as by foreigners. In their surprising 1900 "gastrological" *tour de France*, addressing children, Paul de Courselles and Sixte Delorme wrote:

> Your teachers, whose knowledge and goodwill I do not contest, have certainly said to you that France is the most beautiful country in the world. The most beautiful and the best, do you hear? Because of the diversity of climates, settings, and products. They should have added that no other is so rich in delicacies.[9]

Today, Elizabeth David, the well-known British author of cookbooks, writes for her part, "One of the great characteristics of French cuisine is its extreme variety; it seems to harbor an inexhaustible store of recipes to discover."[10] It is less common to hear an opinion as qualified as that of Joël Robuchon, who, initially an enthusiast, bears in mind that France is not alone in the world:

> It must be said that in France we have food products of exceptional quality as compared to those in all the other countries of the world. Our fruits and vegetables have flavor, our fish is exceptional, as are our creams. We have the world's best butters. That said, good products can also be found in all countries. For example, the ham in Spain is better than in France, Italian olive oil is better than ours. In Japan, Kobe beef is incomparable, and the beef found in the United States is generally excellent, while in France, one in two thousand may be found to be really good. If you don't know your butcher, you won't be well served.[11]

The Gallic and Germanic Inheritance: Rustic Abundance and Sociability

If the secret of the role eating well plays in French culture does not lie in the exceptional character of the country's natural gifts, then it resides in the depths of its inhabitants' imagination.

Without claiming to trace this mindset back to the earliest periods of history, we can note, nonetheless, that it does not contradict the tendencies toward lively sociability and unrestrained sensuality demonstrated by all the "barbaric" populations of Europe, whether of Celtic or Germanic origin.

There is no doubt that certain characteristics of independent Gaul's civilization survived in areas as varied as religion, language, politics, the landscape, the organization of administrative space, etc., despite one cultural tidal wave after another: Roman, Germanic, Italian, Anglo-Saxon, etc. From there, it is not preposterous to hypothesize a link between the marked interest of the Gauls in food and the French gourmand. In Gaul, eating well was inseparable from political and social life. Many texts mention banquets over the course of which great quantities of food and drink were consumed.[12]

Many texts even reveal a veritable bulimia among the Gauls on these occasions. For Athenaeus, drawing from a text by Poseidonios, "their food consists of a small amount of bread and much meat, boiled or cooked over coals or on spits. They are served it properly, but, like lions, take the limbs in both hands and bite into them."[13] And Diodorus of Sicily reveals their penchant for drunkenness:

> Loving wine, they fill up on what the merchants bring without mixing it with water, and, their passion leading them to use drink full strength, they get drunk and sink into sleep or into states of delirium.[14]

It should be noted that drinking undiluted wine is a typical act of "barbarism" in the ancient world,[15] but here we have evidence of the Gallic elite's rapid, enthusiastic adoption of wine consumption, in preparation for the entire population's infatuation with wine growing and wine to follow a bit later.[16] Under Augustus, in the epoch when Diodorus was going back in his writings to the accounts of travelers from preceding centuries, wine was still a luxury:

> Also, many Italian merchants, because of their love for profit, consider the Gauls' penchant for wine a godsend. Bringing wine by boat by using navigable water routes or

> by cart across the plains, they draw an unbelievable price for it: in exchange for a jar of wine, they receive a slave.

Despite this gluttony, which probably was not the everyday norm, the Gauls "watched their figures" and measured themselves regularly with the help of a belt.[17] Moreover, quantity did not preclude the quality of certain preparations, in particular delicatessen products, appreciated as far away as Rome. Strabo declares:

> Such is the number of herds of sheep and pigs that an extraordinary abundance of sausages and salted meats are supplied not only to Rome but to most of the regions of Italy.[18]

Evidence confirmed by Varro:

> The delicatessen products of the Gauls have always been renowned for their excellence and quality. The extensive exportation of hams, sausages, and other preparations of this kind to Rome from this country annually attests to their superiority as well as their flavor.[19]

These tasty salted meats came from the countries of the Séquanes (more or less the Franche-Comté region, still well known for its smoked ham); Narbonnaise, in particular Cerdagne; and the land of the Ménapiens, in Belgian Gaul. We must also mention the geese from the country of the Morins, so prized that they were transported by foot, whole gaggles of them, all the way to Rome, if we are to believe Pliny.[20]

Gaul was already a country exporting cheeses that came from Nîmes, Lozère, Gévaudan, Toulouse, and Tarentaise.[21] The oysters from Bordeaux, Marseilles, and Narbonne were very prized as well, and exported to Italy and Roman Germania.[22]

Should we extrapolate further from this appetizing catalogue and claim that the Gauls had imagined a truly refined cuisine? No. Probably not before the conquest, though their cooking could not have lacked rustic flavor; and if only because there was no body of recipes, indispensable to the creativity and transmission of complex expertise.

From Rome, they learned elaborate methods of food preparation, and they no doubt participated in the development of such methods after their integration into the Empire. What is true of wine aged in the cask is no doubt also true of cooking, at least for the upper classes. For the others, it is difficult to assess the extent to which their diet was modified: eating habits were not the same in the rich Vaison or Comtat plain villas and in the high Diois mountain regions. Where money, culture, and proximity to travel routes allowed, Roman *haute cuisine* was undoubtedly practiced much as it emerges from Apicius's collection *De re coquinaria*, and from all the literature. That being the case, a good meal was copious, even too copious (as before the conquest), but prepared using rare products and following complicated recipes. These have always been the rules for all cuisines developed on earth. Besides the Virgilian meals constituting everyday fare for the Gallo-Roman peasant, the landowner, tradesman, or public official could enjoy oysters, *garum*, pepper, wine from Falerne, and other cosmopolitan delicacies.

Assuming that the Gauls had in part retained their bulimic customs, at least on holidays, the Germanic invasions hardly contradicted them. Even though some of them had already submitted to Roman influence, the invaders had a diet very much resembling that of the long-haired inhabitants of Gaul. Their drink, a product of fermented grain, was also closely related. Bertrand Hell has clearly shown[23] that present-day beer consumption in Alsace, excessive as it often is, is connected to "the importance of libations within the male societies of ancient Germanie, the famous *Männerbunde*."

Taking a beating for a time, wine gradually regained territory through the course of the early Middle Ages, beginning from those centers of viticultural resistance, the episcopal towns and the monasteries. Over the centuries, the country that would become France would never abandon it again, and would make wine the symbol of joy and health, as the religion France embraced invited it to do. The climate did not go against this desire—far from it.

Many authors have tried to explain the flowering of *haute cuisine* in France by the age-old consumption of wine as an accompaniment to food and by its use in the preparation of sauces. This cannot be considered a French monopoly, however, since all the western and southern countries of central Europe, including Great Britain, have produced wine from the Middle Ages to the present without interruption.[24] But surely that factor is not insignificant. The Alsatian chef Emile Jung[25] affirms that a wine sauce offers a complex harmony of acidities leading to perfection. Moreover, wine stimulates the appetite and makes dishes more enticing.[26] With regard to the appetite, that is true of all alcohols, but with regard to enticement, numbing the sense of taste with too high an alcohol content or too strong a component must be avoided. Thus, the bitterness of beer is only acceptable with quite salty or smoked foods; it makes excessively fatty foods tolerable. Brandies and liquors are only useful for digestion and for warmth. Only wines from areas with cold winters, derived from soils where the vine suffers and must draw its nourishment from great depths, developed by wine growers limiting their yields and seeking the highest possible quality, offer the taste buds a gustatory palette sufficiently rich to call for analogous foods. For various reasons, France has gradually gained a leading position in matters of quality wines. Cooking is closely intermingled with that phenomenon: the two techniques took off and developed in concert with each other since the eighteenth century.[27]

Are French and Regional Cuisines a Recent Invention?

During the Middle Ages, it seems France was hardly distinguishable from the rest of Europe as far as diet was concerned, whether it was a matter of ordinary everyday or extraordinary fare. That is the opinion of many authors and also of Stephan Mennell, who has compared England and France in minute detail: "With diet as with many other aspects of the Middle Ages, the difference is much more clear between the social strata of one country than between the countries themselves."[28] If that is the case at the level of countries, it is *a fortiori* the case at the level of regions. The geographer faces the same problem here as he does with regard to landscape: the great bocage–open field–wooded landscape divisions of southern France only clearly appear at the end of the Middle Ages and are not really complete until the eighteenth century,[29] but that doesn't rule out earlier subtle variations that current documentation does not allow us to fully apprehend. The same is true for languages, the architecture of rural houses, and clothing. We must mistrust both those boundaries presented as very clear cut and old and those comparisons too easily drawn. Cultural space, as fluid and capricious as societies, is very tricky to map with confidence in earlier periods. It is likely, however, that it reached its greatest diversity only on the eve of industrial standardization in the mid- or late nineteenth century.

Therefore, lacking more precise information, we can assume that French and European peasants in the Middle Ages and the centuries that followed usually consumed food of vegetable origin resulting from cultivation or gathering. The base of their diet was bread, made from wheat in the best cases, but usually made from rye, barley, or mixed grains, with greater or lesser quantities of bran added to it. White bread was a delicacy most peasants never tasted. The dark-colored round loaves, made of more or less well-risen dough according to the nature of the flour and the caprices of the leavening, were imposing in size, so that they would keep a long time—a week or even longer. Thus bread was eaten stale, which was hardly a problem since it served first of all to soak up soup, the veritable national dish for France and even Europe.

This soup simmered for a long time at the hearth, in a clay or cast-iron pot set on a tripod or hanging on a trammel. Besides more or less questionable water from a well or a river, and best when it came from a spring, what was it made of? Chiefly vegetables: cabbage, beans, various "roots" (rutabagas, carrots, turnips, leeks), bulbs (onions, garlic, muscaris), cultivated or wild herbs such as chives, parsley, nettle, wild thyme, sage, etc. Most of the time, it contained no meat element, or if so, only a piece of salt pork meant to flavor everything. Insofar as possible, it was enriched with a bit of pork, beef, sheep, or goose fat (or all mixed together, as in the well-known *graisse normande* soup), milk, cream, butter, or oil (walnut or olive oil, for example).

Otherwise, peasants ate more or less thick cereal gruels, a food familiar since the Neolithic and still eaten widely today on every continent.[30] Crêpes and *galettes* are only variations developed from such gruels. Cheese and dairy products were commonly used, but in limited quantities; often, the full-fat cheese was sold, and peasants ate only the buttermilk by-products (*cancoillote* from the Jura, similar to Welsh Rarebit, is a vestige of this that has resisted the food revolution). On Sunday, the soup was enlivened with a bit more salt pork or, more rarely, a fowl when the farm's stores, the egg demand, and feudal taxes allowed one to be sacrificed. As for drink, it was mostly water, supplemented to whatever possible extent by wine, cider, or some other fruit-based local brew (like the ones that still very much survive in England, called "wines").

The theory of spatial uniformity is well illustrated by the Provençal example studied by Louis Stouff and Jacques Barrau.[31] The tomato-garlic-olive oil triad, which passes for characteristic of that region and differentiates it from the rest of France, is actually very recent, and not only because of the tomato, originally American. In a study of the Provençal diet in the fourteenth and fifteenth centuries, Louis Stouff demonstrates that it relied upon cabbage, supplemented by leeks, beans, spinach, and lettuce, which tradition claims was introduced by the popes but which surely goes back much further.

> The consumption of olive oil, he notes, the use of garlic, the predominance of mutton, and a certain taste for aromatic plants are what delight those who celebrate a legendary Provence. . . . What is true for the twentieth and nineteenth centuries is not necessarily true for the late Middle Ages. At that time, it seems, oil was only used for eggs and fish, or for fried beans. Outside of these few dishes, salt pork was the preferred fat for soups. Pea, bean, and cabbage soup with lard was the staple food of peasants, artisans and the simple folk of Provence.[32]

As the Provençal example goes on, we can see that many so-called "regional" dishes only exist thanks to the introduction of

American vegetables. That is so with regard to green peppers and *pipérade*, foie gras and corn, cassoulet and beans, *gratin dauphinois* or *potée* and potatoes. This phenomenon is identical in foreign countries: what would Italian cooking be without the tomato?

According to Jean-Louis Flandrin, however, uniformity was not as marked as some historians believe.[33] Without falling back on the myth of antiquity and the durability of regional cuisines, he notes that as early as the end of the Middle Ages, cookbooks—reflecting the dietary habits of the aristocracy—testify not only to a real cosmopolitanism but also to gustatory idiosyncrasies:

> In all of them, we find Oriental spices, verjuice, slightly sour or bittersweet flavors, a near absence of fatty sauces, contempt for butter and green vegetables, emphasis on roasted poultry and game, fish on Fridays, bread and grain dishes. But behind this superficial uniformity, more careful study reveals national and regional tastes: different ranges of spices, contrasts between English boiled onions and French or Italian fried onions, between the Italian, Catalan, and especially English taste for sweet or bittersweet flavors and the French taste for a sharp acidity, etc.

He mentions regional names like "*tarte bourbonnoise,*" "*brouet de Savoie,*" "*sauce cameline à la façon de Tournai,*" etc.

Over the course of the centuries, the peasant diet was spatially enriched and diversified. Starches began to be used to supplement or even replace bread when the grain harvests were insufficient: chestnuts in areas with acid soils, beans that came from America as early as the sixteenth century, potatoes in the eighteenth century after a long purgatory. The swine population benefited from the latter, and the piece of lard in the soup pot grew. One type of grain, also American, that is, corn, allowed for the preparation of substantial porridges in the southwest (*millat*) and Bresse (*gaudes*), but especially for the intensification of poultry farming, indeed even the fattening of poultry. With the eighteenth–nineteenth century revolution in feed, livestock were more abundant and better nourished, and the consumption of meat became less of a rarity. Among the well-to-do peasants (the farmers) of the castles or among the artisans and merchants of the towns, that rich and flavorful, so-called "earthy" cuisine gradually developed, still the glory of many French provinces: daubes, ragoûts, cassoulets, *saupiquets*, *potées*, rich in meat, wine sauces, and cream. This cuisine did not disdain updating and preserving older practices. *Pot-au-feu*, the enriched ancestor of cabbage soup, transformed into a veritable national dish, is one example, as Brillat-Savarin attests, evoking eighteenth-century meals: "Between noon and one o'clock, we dine on the official *potage* and *pot-au-feu*, more or less well accompanied according to fortune and circumstance."[34]

From the beginning, holiday abundance offered a contrast to the rusticity and the restrictions ordinarily imposed upon the vast majority, whether it was a matter of agrarian holidays or holidays related to the liturgical calendar or the cycle of the year. It was then that calves, cows, pigs, and poultry were sacrificed, that the cured meats hanging from the ceiling or in the chimney were taken down, and that the cask of wine or cider saved for the occasion was tapped. All the products usually sold in town or given as taxes to the lord were consumed without restraint: wheat flour, eggs, butter, oil, cheese. Not many herbs or root vegetables on those days, but meat, a profusion of meats, consolation for the too light or too sugary everyday fare. Until the 1970s, in all French countrysides, the killing of a pig gave rise to a feast over the course of which you stuffed yourself with meat, a phenomenon that can still be observed in many poor countries. It is difficult to fathom the quantity of mutton or camel meat that a Moor, used to living most days on practically nothing, can consume on a holiday. Until very recently, country wedding feasts lasted for hours and often extended over many days.[35] At the beginning of this century, the folklorist Van Gennep studied and compared them a great deal:

> From the menus we have, dating from the Middle Ages to about the end of the eighteenth century, it becomes clear that the preference was given to game. In our day, game only appears during the authorized hunting periods or as a result of poaching. A small wedding in Vendée included an "opening dish" of sixty hens and chickens; elsewhere, over the course of large weddings involving one hundred to five hundred people, the meat consisted of mutton, veal, pork, and even entire beef. . . . As for liquid refreshments, they must flow without limit, and the cupbearer's job is to pour drinks until the casks of cider and wine are empty and the guests perfectly saturated.[36]

As we can see, the Gallic traditions reported by Athenaeus and Diodorus or those of the Germanic world remained alive and well! Very simply, no moral authority ever truly and definitively condemned them.

All the same, until the twentieth century, everyday country fare remained quite meager on the whole. Not by choice, certainly, but by necessity, and that is why euphoric abundance had so strong a hold upon imaginations.

The Rabelaisian Spirit of the French

Thus, over the centuries, the French have alternated among habitual frugality, fasts and abstinences imposed by the Church, and outright unrestrained drunken feasts. Far from passing over these latter in silence or condemning them, all of popular culture has glorified, embellished, and lauded them in stories, poems, songs, and proverbs, associating the belly's holiday with that of all the senses. There is no difference between the bawdy Gallic and the Rabelaisian, both mixtures of pleasure, raciness, and good-natured hospitality ending in, if necessary, actual fistfights. This cultural context is essential for understanding how *haute cuisine* was born, no matter how far removed from that coarse abundance it seems.

As Pierre Jourda has demonstrated,[37] there is some realism in Rabelais's Gargantua, totally in keeping with medieval fabliaux and farces. The dispute between the Fats and the Thins is a theme direct from a twelfth-century poem entitled "*Bataille de Carême et Mange-Viande*" ("Battle of Lent and Meat-Eater").[38] From this hyperbole and witty eloquence emanates a formidable optimism, one of the oldest elements in Western societies and one that French society will maintain quite well. Thus, in attempting to demonstrate the popular and medieval roots of Rabelais's work, Mikhail Bakhtine wrote:

> This encounter with the world through the absorption of food was joyous and triumphant. Man triumphed over the world, swallowed it instead of being swallowed by it. . . . Rabelais was completely convinced that one could only express the truth freely and frankly in the ambiance of the banquet, and only in the tones of dinner conversation.[39]

If the glorification of stuffing oneself disappeared from literature over the course of the modern epoch, the idea that friendship and sincerity are inseparable from the well-lubricated banquet has survived to our day. We find it offered in many forms among "gastrosophers" such as Berchoux and Brillat-Savarin.[40]

We might be tempted to believe that Rabelaisian excess and its ancestor, Gallic bawdiness, are specialties exclusive to the French. Not in the least. These ways of approaching life can also be found in Petronius's *Satyricon*, as in all the literature and popular theater of medieval Europe. Consider Boccaccio's *Decameron*, all of the *Commedia dell'Arte*, or Chaucer's *Canterbury Tales*. The excesses of the carnival may differ in style of expression but not in intensity, as we can see today in Brazil or in the Caribbean, where its spirit has survived and prospered.

In the sixteenth century, all of Europe still experienced the shared joys and pleasures of stuffing oneself to the gills, which its literature still openly conveys. Sancho Panza and Falstaff, grotesque characters, no doubt, but so true and so human, are Gargantua's close companions. But with the dawn of the individual conscience, the pessimism lying in wait for the West was already present. Until then, the Church had kept it in check. With the modern epoch, it washed over every part of Europe. France, like Italy, would be spared for the most part and would retain excessive eating and drinking as an essential component of its identity.

Chapter Two

Is Gourmandism a Sin in France?

FOR THE LOVE OF EATING well to be so widespread in France, the moral authorities must have ignored or even encouraged this penchant throughout the period of its development. That is the hypothesis maintained here; but things are not so simple, as is the case in all civilizations, when it comes to the question of putting the senses to good use. It is unusual for strict prohibitions or limitations aimed at condemning the offender to be applied to all manifestations of sensuality for an entire population over a long period of time. Often moralists realistically provide escape valves. It seems as though gourmandism has played this role in France. The attitude of the clergy, ambiguous and varying over time but rather lax overall, obviously has had something to do with this. Moreover, that attitude is true for the whole Roman Catholic Church, where a convenient interpretation of the Holy Scriptures has prevailed on this point.

Did Jesus Love to Eat?

In matters of food and drink, the Old Testament very markedly glorifies temperance and asceticism. Of course, there is Noah's intoxication, but that is presented more as a result of the patriarch's ignorance about the effects of wine and as a lesson on filial morality than as an example to follow. The manna in the desert is delicious food, but it is not a matter of skillful culinary preparation, any more than are the milk and honey running freely in the land of Canaan or the fruits in the garden of Eden. Nonetheless, gastronomy is not absent. As nomadic peoples of the Sahara and the Middle East still do today, the Hebrews could undoubtedly prepare incomparable roast lamb, and all the references to fatted calves attest to the existence of special livestock raised for important occasions. It is likely that much eating and drinking took place during such celebrations. And then, of course, there is the Song of Songs, where all the senses are exalted, including taste, and put to the service of glorifying God.

Everything leads us to think that Christ did not try to distinguish himself from this sober though not overly restrictive culture, not considering those prohibitions particular to Judaism. Certainly, he continually called for penitence and detachment from worldly goods, and he warned, "Take heed so that your hearts are not weighted down with dissipation and drunkenness."[1] But he himself did not live anything like his cousin, John the Baptist, who fed on grasshoppers, or like the Desert Fathers would have to, or like the Carthusian monks! On the contrary, outside of the fasting periods to which he subjected himself (the forty days in the desert, for example), he liked to eat and even to eat well. His words, reported by two evangelists, are proof of that:

> For John came, neither eating nor drinking, and they say, "He is possessed!" The Son of man came, eating and drinking, and they say, "Behold a glutton and a drunkard, a friend of tax collectors and sinners!" But Wisdom is justified by her deeds.[2]

As for the episode involving the wedding at Cana (to which wine lovers may appeal a bit too often), it certainly has major theological significance, but the miracle Christ performs comes about through an excellent wine, so fine that a connoisseur is surprised that the master of the house waited for the end of the meal to serve it, since the guests' minds were already cloudy and their taste buds saturated.

In his recent book, *Jésus*, Jean-Paul Roux arrives at the same conclusions:

> He eats and drinks wine, goes to celebrations and weddings when he is invited. He is called a "drunkard and a glutton," which is not necessarily true, but which the evangelist reveals without shame. He doesn't refuse a good meal. He shares lunch with the Pharisees and the publicans, men who, we cannot doubt, knew how to entertain and took much trouble in doing so.[3]

Certain exegeses have presented Jesus as austere and hieratic. It is very often said that Christ never laughed. That is possible, if we do not go beyond the letter of the texts, all silent on this point, but nevertheless he recommended laughing with those who laugh. Why wouldn't he have followed his own advice addressed to his disciples?

Behind this question of what pleasure Jesus derived from eating and drinking emerges all the theology of the Incarnation. For a Christian, Christ, truly God and truly man, cannot have escaped the appeal of the senses. The texts lead us to believe that he remained chaste but also that he clearly suffered temptations. "To help us," wrote Saint Paul, "we have a pontiff who can sympathize with our weaknesses, having been tempted and tested Himself in all things."[4] It diminishes his humanity to imagine him stone cold facing Mary Magdalene or in a few other circumstances.

Totally human, Christ felt the appeal of all the senses, and quite evidently felt pleasure and distaste. He loved the scent of the myrrh and incense offered by the wise men those first days of his infancy and the prize perfume Mary Magdalene used on his feet. He loved the caress of the courtesan's hair, the caress of pure water from the Jordan and the Sea of Galilee, of his tunic's finely woven linen against his skin, of wood planed smooth in Joseph's workshop. He loved the song of the desert wind and the one he heard in the synagogues. Finally, he loved his Cana wine and the wine of the Last Supper, which could not have tasted foul, as did that mixture of vinegar and gall presented to him on the cross. How crusty and well risen the bread to feed the multitudes must have been, and how divinely grilled the fish distributed that day, since they were prepared in the celestial kitchens! No doubt Christ knew how to discern the essence of Creation behind what he ate and drank and how to immediately see into the heart of the one who had cooked it or harvested the grapes, impressions too fleeting for common mortals but that, when they arise, provide the gastronome with unspeakable joy. To be convinced of this, we only need recall certain dishes we used to love, the beloved who prepared them having departed.

The First Christians and Food

From the beginning, Christians distinguished themselves from Jews by no longer respecting the dietary prohibitions of the Mosaic Law, and the Church in the earliest centuries never legislated on this subject, apart from the fasts and abstinences. Moreover, bread and wine are at the heart of the Eucharistic celebration, that is, at the heart of Christianity. To read Saint Paul, we could even think that very early on, gourmandism was placed among the ranks of venial sins: "Foods is meant for the stomach and the stomach for food, and God will destroy one and the other. But the body is not meant for fornication; it is for the Lord, and the Lord for the body."[5] Strange, even specious, this distinction between the belly and what lies below the belly, but the die are cast; henceforth there will be a double standard; the excesses of eating well are not penalized in the same way as those of sexuality. The Church later listed gluttony, like lust, among the seven deadly sins,[6] that is, the vices capable of leading to others, which does not mean they are mortal. A sin can be both deadly and . . . sweet, that is, venial.

The evangelical message clearly grants more importance to the spirit than to the letter of the law, the nit-picking provisions. Humans being what they are, however, the Church prescribed a certain number of moral regulations, organized sins into a hierarchy, and posted the punishments. Its demands in these matters varied with time and place, as a function of the nature of populations and attitudes. Rigorous asceticism is one path recommended from the very beginning, in the tradition of John the Baptist, the last of the prophets, but it is not required of all the faithful. To each his own. . . .

The first centuries' saints already proposed all the possible paths for experiencing the senses, and especially taste, in a Christian way. There is the path of total renunciation, which is the path of the Desert Fathers, the anchorites like Saint Anthony, and the three Saint Simeon Stylites who lived on a column. Hermeticism has continued until the twentieth century, illustrated, for example, by Charles de Foucauld. An ideal path, but so difficult, judging by the temptations suffered by those who choose it! This current has religious roots in Judaism, but also in pagan philosophy. The stoics, who did not, for all that, renounce their social life, exemplified it for centuries, from Zenon (third century B.C.) to Epictetus (first century A.D.) and Marcus Aurelius (second century). In his *Manual*, Epictetus writes:

> Only take what is strictly necessary for attending to the body: food, drink, clothing, house, servants; all that is for show or for comfort, totally abolish. . . . It is a mark of impotence if too much importance is given to the cares of the body, to gymnastics, food, drink, natural functions; all that must be considered secondary and all the attention must go to the mind.[7]

But there is also some advice in Epictetus that could fall into the category of Christian charity: "A certain [. . .] drinks much wine: do not say that is bad, say that they drink much wine. Because before knowing the reasons, how do you know if it is bad?"

It was to better combat the temptations inherent in hermeticism that Saint Benoît—as others before him, but with mixed success—codified communal life in the sixth century. The rule is harsh and proclaims, "Death is located at the same entry as pleasure,"[8] but insofar as food was concerned, it reveals itself to be fundamentally very flexible.[9] If the keeper of the wine cellar must be austere in his habits, the monks are invited not to overexert themselves. In particular, Benoît advises them to go without wine if they can, but if not, a *hémine* (.27 liter/8 ounces) per day is kindly granted. In the absence of statistics on their consumption, let us wager that many Benedictines must have chosen the second solution, if only because the Roman legacy survived in many regions thanks to those monasteries and because wine producing was one of the most remarkable points of Roman resistance within barbarian Europe.[10] The Benedictine rule represents a middle path in matters of food.

On the other side of the path to perfection, we encounter the good bishop of Poitiers, the late sixth-century Saint Fortunat (Venantius Fortunatus), honored in our day by Father Maurice Lelong with the title of "the patron of big eaters."[11] He was full heir to the Roman culture in its least austere but also most Christian version. Leaving Ravenna, where he had studied, about 565, he set out on a pilgrimage to Tours, and during the two years his journey lasted, he stayed with various hosts, civil and religious, turning out verses for their benefit as a way of thanking them for their hospitality.

To Gogon, the Sigebert palace mayor, he wrote:[12]

> Nectar, wines, dishes, clothing, learning, fortune! You are enough to me, Gogon, without all that. You are both the generous Cicero and Apicius my compatriot; you satisfy me with beautiful language and nourish me with good things to eat. But I ask for your grace; my stomach is stuffed full of beef and I must collect myself.

To Mummolenus, a rich inhabitant of Soissons, he describes the banquet offered him by the ex-queen of the Franks, the future Saint Radegonde, abbess of the Saint-Croix de Poitiers monastery, where he is chaplain:

> Plates filled to the brim with exquisite dishes rose from the table like hills. The table seemed like a valley to me with the tablecloth for sod, bordered by a ravine having for a river streams of oil in which fish swam. First I was presented with sweet fruits commonly called peaches. There was no end to the food and no end to my eating. . . . Soon my stomach stuck out like a woman's about to give birth; I admire the extent to which this organ can stretch. There were groans of thunder in mine with the various attempts to suppress them; the winds from the north and the south wreaked havoc with my entrails.[13]

The ways of the Lord are inscrutable, and Fortunat's immoderate passion for eating well did not stand in the way of his canonization. He is the true founder of a very Christian gourmandism, in the French style, that only came under attack locally or temporarily in the centuries following.

These three methods for drawing close to God, the austere, the middle way, and the merry, all of which were practiced and still are today throughout the Christian world, nevertheless shared one essential point in the Church's first centuries: their fundamental optimism. Everyone can benefit from the Redemption provided that they have faith, hope, and charity, that is, love for God. Whether you stuff your belly or live off grasshoppers makes little difference, considering the overabundance of grace. Throughout the Middle Ages, we find this unity again in the diversity of rules on lifestyle, in France as elsewhere, except at the times and in the areas of certain heresies peddling pessimistic visions of the world.

Christian Faith and Eating Well in the Middle Ages

Skimming through the texts mentioning pleasure, especially the pleasures of the table in the medieval period, we might believe we are dealing with followers of different religions; this is not at all the case. Moral theology continues to waver between a strict attitude, praising mastery over the senses and associated with penitence, and another, more common and comfortably lax, maintaining that many things are more important in religion and that the pleasures of the table, well tempered, can even elevate the soul.

Among the adherents of the first view looms the tall, combative figure of Saint Bernard, defender of austere observance of the Benedictine rule. That did not prevent the Cîteaux abbey, lost in the marshes and the fogs of the Saône plain, from promoting a high-quality viticulture at the Vougeot vineyard it owned on the Gold Coast, where it produced one of the truly premier *grands crus* in the history of France.[14] The co-planting of fruit trees was suspended. The wall enclosing the domain protected the vines from livestock and retained heat. The pressing and wine-making processes underwent remarkable refinements. Why so much effort? First of all, for the greater glory of God; in that, the Cistercians hardly differed from the Clunisians, who focused all their attention on architectural opulence and decoration. Second, because wine served to honor distinguished visitors; the abbot drank it with his guests and had it served to his monks on special occasions. In the cloistered life, as pious and stringent as it was, occasional permission to taste a great wine left a lasting impression prompting one to anticipate the next such occasion with more or less impatience and providing delicious food for thought. Overall, it still remained true that the Cistercians lived very abstemiously, just like the Carthusians, who followed a middle path between hermeticism and conventional life but who, with the produce from the tiny plot of land each cultivated, had little opportunity for feasting.

This was not the case in all the monasteries. In the twelfth century, Julien de Vézelay described the dietary regime of the monks in this way:

> They get drunk on many wines, the source of lust; they gorge themselves on meat when they are neither sick nor anemic, but for their pleasure alone and without any need for it; they claim rights to the supplementary diet our Father Benoît allowed only for healing sickness and anemia. The monastery's everyday fare is not good enough for them, and while Jerome grants the monk only a few small fish, they find even the large fish brought as tribute insufficient. They pounce on meat, to the point that a monk can no longer be distinguished from a layperson judging from their diets, but only thanks to their robes.[15]

During the Middle Ages, gourmandism is very often stigmatized by preachers, and this is true throughout the Western world, relatively poorly differentiated from this perspective. Here is an English example from the fourteenth century, drawn from the treatise on penitence that Chaucer has the parson speak at the end of the *Canterbury Tales*:

> Gluttony has corrupted the world, as the sin of Adam and Eve shows. It has many branches, the first of which is drunkenness, which is "the sepulture of human reason." Here are the others, according to Saint Gregory: "The first is to eat before the hours; the second is to seek out fine

meat and drink; the third is to eat beyond measure, the fourth is curiosity about dressing meats; the fifth is eating gluttonously. These are the five fingers of the devil's hand, by means of which he lures men to sin."[16]

In the fifteenth century, the great French rhetorician Jean Molinet also condemned eating well without calling it by name:

Par faulx regard, langue friande,
Bouche trop gloute et trop truande
Tant en parler comme en viande,
Notre povre âme, vile et orde,
Le cours de raison se desborde.

(By false regard, fond tongue,
Mouth too greedy and too crooked
As much for speaking as for meat,
Our poor soul, vile and filthy,
The course of reason overflows.)[17]

In order for such condemnations to be repeated throughout the centuries, there must be real grounds, and we have many examples of monasteries where life flows sweetly, not to mention the overflows of which lay society is so fond. Michel Rouche has shown[18] that these practices are very old. In the Carolingian epoch, in certain abbeys, the kings instituted very lavish banquets—called *consolationes refectionis*—provided to the monks and intended to celebrate the anniversaries the monarchs held dear: the birth of princes, ancestors, wives, their coronations, and various noteworthy events in their reigns. The purpose was clear: the special meal was a propitiatory rite meant to ensure the dynasty's continuation. It was a matter of "legitimizing their power, as if those sacred feasts had a mysterious aggregative force over divine power. . . . And the hypothesis comes to mind that, since these practices appeared in Germanic countries, behind their official Christianity, they are distantly related in some way to brotherhood revels and pagan rites during which constraints (dietary or sexual) were lifted, thus calling for a celebration of fertility (spiritual or carnal)."[19]

What is striking geographically about these abbeys is that they are essentially distributed throughout the wealthy regions forming the heart of Carolingian power, those places where, in 802, Charlemagne permanently established the *missi dominici*: Paris, Soissons, Reims, Orléans, Mâcon. Still today, the heart of the Parisian basin and the Saône valley and its borders are regions of exceptionally well-developed gastronomy, both traditional and modern.

These Carolingian meals clearly laid the foundations for the gastronomic moral doctrine in France; the passion for eating well was associated with what all men, whether princes, monks, or simple mortals, hold most dear: praising God; public order guaranteed by the continuity of families or dynasties; fraternal conviviality; a respect for the body and its needs—at the very least, its dietary ones; the legitimacy of certain pleasures. They also prefigured the close ties that would later be established between the central power and gastronomic creativity.

The Church attempted to curb these monastic practices that testify to a very optimistic conception of Christianity, without much success, as we have seen. Many monasteries maintained a very high level of culinary—and oenological—expertise until the Revolution, probably not only for the purposes of entertaining their visiting dignitaries but also for the simple pleasure of sharing a good meal. As E. Charbonnier has explained so well, "Detached from a certain number of material cares, and removed from other temptations, monks often let themselves go when it came to eating well—*gastimargia* and *gula*."[20]

The Defeat of Catharist Asceticism

The episode of Catharism with its dramatic close is very revealing of French reservations with regard to the most pessimistic and austere models, in this case involving an experiment influenced by eastern religions.

We know that the doctrine of Manes, which inspired Catharism,[21] was first conceived in Persia in the third century. It held that the devil created the human body and that humans must thus detach themselves as early as possible from their carnal nature, by definition evil. Toward that end, the most extreme asceticism had to be practiced. It was forbidden to promote or perpetuate the empire of evil through human, animal, or plant reproduction. As it is impossible to put such principles into general practice, a distinction then developed between the elect or "pure"—the future "perfect" of Catharism—for whom paradise was reserved and who practiced a rigorous asceticism, and the "believers," who ensured the subsistence of the elect. The believers were reincarnated after their deaths in a more or less honorable way within the human or animal realm, as a function of merit earned during their lives. The only hope of escaping this wandering about in successive reincarnations was to be reborn someday among the "pure."

Manicheanism had not disappeared from the East, Armenia in particular, but also Bulgaria where the Bogomils were its heirs. Bogomilism spread along the Dalmatian coast and from there filtered into northern Italy. In all of the Christian East, where dualism existed, latent, for a long time, we find many Manicheans called Cathari—from the Greek *catharos*, pure—

beginning in the eleventh century. Theirs was a total renunciation, at least for the "perfect." They did not kill animals or eat meat. The wine that they drank in moderation was so heavily cut with water that it hardly retained its taste.[22]

The geographical problem they pose is complex. How was it possible for such a pessimistic religion to attract followers in the south of France, among the descendants of the Romanized and then Germanized Gauls, heirs to many traditions much more serene and joyous even for those adhering to an austerity for which the Christian ideal is unobtrusive self-denial? Maybe we could apply to Catharism the hypothesis Emmanual Todd defends with regard to Protestantism:[23]

> The latter, for which the conception of salvation is fundamentally determinist—just as it is already with Catharism—flourishes mostly in the regions with inegalitarian dynastic families, precisely the system to which all of southwest France belongs.
>
> Protestant predestination, the idea of an omnipotent God and of men being unequal with regard to salvation, was accepted easily where there pre-existed a familial organization composed of an authoritarian father and unequal brothers, that is, in the countries with dynastic families.[24]

Renouncing the pleasures of the senses, indeed even the simple use of them, becomes the norm in so unjust a context, where the father has the right to pass on the inheritance or not, as God has the right to save or damn, regardless of merit. Under such duress, one can lose a taste for life. Fernand Niel is surprised by the contrast between Catharism and the troubadour poetry that flourished in the same region at the same time.[25] Denis Rougemont provides the key to this mystery by showing[26] that this poetry, while appearing to be light, is in fact stamped with a fatal pessimism that could be summarized thus: "there is no happy love." How could it be otherwise when this life is only considered a vale of tears? Moreover, in this literature, the heroes' stomachs are hardly more satisfied than their hearts. "Love draws the hero in so well that he no longer eats or sleeps. Is that serious? Not at all. Love is enough; no need to dine. . . . In general, the time for a meal is time wasted, time to leisurely describe the contents of a meal is time wasted."[27]

Nevertheless, we must not give too much weight to this appealing explanation. Why didn't southwestern France remain austere at the end of the Inquisition's repression? It must be that the optimistic Roman tradition was the stronger one, even if this region later somewhat favored the Reformation. And also, with regard to food, it may be that the dynastic family system created quality and refinement, thanks to daughters, mothers, and grandmothers all living under the same roof, thus allowing for culinary expertise to be passed along under optimal conditions.

Was the Protestant Reformation Antigastronomic?

The Reformation was a key period for gastronomy and for the way it subsequently spread throughout Europe. One of its main concerns was to criticize the lavish customs adopted by a whole segment of the clergy. Luther categorically condemns luxury, whether the Church's or lay society's:

> There is hardly any order these days at the tables of princes or in the management of their houses. . . . In our times, to maintain the vain, disorderly lavishness of the

> banquets and feasts of the brotherhoods, four imperial cities waste in one day more than was spent in a month in the entire expanse of Solomon's estates.[28]

He even makes remarks that would lead us to believe he was a strict vegetarian, an idea we find again later in Rousseau:

> "It is certain," said Doctor Luther one day, holding in his hand a root thick with juice, "that the patriarchs' only foods were fruits and roots. I am convinced that Adam truly relished these dishes, and that he never considered eating a partridge."[29]

But everyone has his contradictions, and this is the same man who exclaims in 1538: "Let him be pitied, that ill-favored man whose wife or servant understands nothing about cooking! This misfortune in housekeeping is the source of many ills."[30] It is true that there is a difference between mere cooking and eating well, and that Martin Luther's sensual propensities did not prevent the Reformation, first the Lutheran, and then the Calvinist, from opting for austerity.

The causes are multiple and convergent. Criticism of the Church, too attached to worldly possessions, must be given primary importance. This was an ancient tradition going back to the first centuries of Christianity, and, as we have seen, the reformers unfaithful to Rome were not consistent for long, even though moderation remained characteristic of Protestant populations. To understand why, we must consider the moral attitude of the Protestants in relationship to their eliminating the sacrament of penitence, thus obliging them to remain on the alert—maintaining the faithful in a state of permanent anxiety. Among the Calvinists and the Puritans, predestination heightened this tendency. It pushed the faithful toward work and business, success implying salvation,[31] but not toward the consumption of the goods thus earned. "In idleness," writes Philippe Besnard, "the faithful one would lose all proof of his election; that is why enjoying worldly goods, relaxing with one's possessions, is reprehensible, much more so than acquiring riches resulting from methodical, unrelenting work."[32] Among the Protestants who rejected predestination (Pietists, Methodists, Baptists), there is an "obligation for the faithful one to control his state of grace through ascetic conduct and a rationalized existence."[33] Only a totally controlled life, in effect, allows one to escape the cycle consisting of friendship with God–failure–sacramental reconciliation.

We must also mention the Protestant perspective on the world. Creation and the supernatural no longer communicate. Thus the possibility of making food sacred, of drawing a bit closer to God by eating good things—that old animist idea that Christianity had more or less taken over as its own—disappears. And finally, the importance of reading and meditating personally upon the Holy Scriptures directed Protestants toward matters of the mind, and the whole history of humanity shows intellectuals in general to be less inclined toward sensuality than intuitive types are.

Nevertheless, today there are many Protestants attached to good food and good wines. They number among them the Lutherans of Alsace and the German Rhine. There is not a trace of ascetic mortification, for example, among the great Haeberlin d'Illhaeusern cooks or among their friends, the Hugels, wine growers, both father and son, for three and a half centuries, who make some of Alsace's best wines in Riquewihr.

The attitude is more ambiguous in the Chartrons families in Bordeaux and the Cognac wine merchants. A certain number of them have English ancestry or come from various Protestant northern European countries. In these noble houses, every attempt is made to obtain the highest quality wines possible. They have the expertise, and they know how to appreciate good and beautiful things, but with sensible moderation. They never abandon themselves completely, and if they give way to excess on occasion, it is because they have been taken by surprise. That great and pious lady of Médoc whose family formerly came from Denmark speaks of her wine elegantly and mentions in moving but restrained terms the pleasure of wiping the corners of her mouth on damask linen, starched by hand, after having sampled the boned thrush in *chaud-froid* sauce prepared by her grandmother's cook. . . .

Théodore Monod, a great figure in liberal French Protestantism, pushes the paradox even further. A detached scholar, he traveled about the Sahara on a camel throughout his life, carrying only rice and his Bible. Nevertheless, in response to a journalist who asked him a little naively if there were a link between the call of the spirit and the call of the desert, he recently declared, "A meharist in the middle of the desert thinks about a big glass of lemonade and a piece of Camembert. Not very metaphysical, you see."[34] You can't mix God and the desert, and this totally prosaic retort seeks to clearly distinguish the domain of earthly realities from the Almighty's. All the same, the combination Théodore Monod suggests is not very gastronomic!

One final example, from very stringent Norway. In September 1989, during the centennial celebration of the Geographic Society in Oslo, a sober banquet presided over by King Olav V ended with an infinite number of speeches. The last was an interminable elaboration on the several dishes and drinks just served. This is, apparently, a tradition. And a surprising one, frankly, since in France propriety forbids any talk at the table about what is being eaten—a prohibition, we might as well admit, that the majority of French people willingly violate!

Beyond that, all evidence seems to grant the Protestant Reformation a definite air of sobriety, even renunciation. We must put aside the question of Protestants not practicing fasts and abstinence and thus passing momentarily for "gourmands" among the Catholics. This is much more a matter of debate over religious sincerity (can one truly respect the law and still eat lobster or dinosaur eggs on Friday?) than over pleasure.

In France, Sully was one of the first defenders of Calvinist severity. He greatly valued honors and pensions, obvious signs of God's favor, but congratulated himself on never caring for "delicacies, sauces, pastries, jams, fancy meats, drunkenness, gluttony, nor the riffraff at long, overflowing tables."[35] Plow and pasture are only meant for producing food, not for making life more pleasant or for helping the vale of tears to flourish. Moreover, his Henrichemont project was to create a perfect society through an ideal town plan, not a Théleme abbey. Thus, the case grounded on clichés hostile to Protestantism is not a false one, much later leading L. Vitet to write in *La Mort d'Henri III*:

> THE KING—It's strange, in truth; but I cannot imagine that I should never again enter Paris . . . !
>
> D'EPERON—Sire, you have the keys to it hanging from your belt.
>
> THE KING—But those Huguenots, my child . . . !
>
> D'EPERON—They will return to Saintonge to eat their dark bread; and we, Sire, we will go to dine at Lemore's and at Samson's, we will eat elaborate ragoûts. . . . Twenty pistols per head . . . marzipan, gherkins, sugar-coated almonds *à la d'Aumale*.[36]

Over the course of the seventeenth and eighteenth centuries in France and throughout northern Europe, the Reformation became firmly entrenched for the reasons already indicated. And if the English Puritans had "a passion for happiness," as Edmund Leites has tried to demonstrate,[37] their doctrine nevertheless transformed

> merry old England into a more sober and more stable world. . . . Self-control, moderation, and the relentless pursuit of spiritual and moral objectives seemed to them the necessary and essential expression of religious dignity and an awareness of God. . . . They did not seek out asceticism, but, though not a prescriptive ideal, a certain level of asceticism was no less a psychological reality, unfortunately.[38]

Unruly and excessive behavior, court holidays when you indulged in earthly sustenance without restraint—in short, all that inconstancy the Middle Ages loved so much henceforth found itself falling into line across the Channel as in the rest of Protestant Europe. We can only appreciate Voltaire's irony when he asserts:

> Compared to a young and lively French bachelor squawking in the theology schools in the morning, and singing with the ladies in the evening, an Anglican theologian is a Cato; but even this Cato seems like a gallant suitor compared to a Scottish Presbyterian. . . . These gentlemen, who also have a few churches in England, have made solemn airs the fashion in that country.[39]

Cooking felt the effects of this, and Stephen Mennell is very much alone in his attempt to defend the English gentry's cuisine, so much simpler than that of the French nobility in the eighteenth century: "These people ate in the English style because they liked it."[40] That much is obvious, but it is not an explanation.

On the other hand, it is no different among the Calvinists. "If an emblematic figure of renunciation in gastronomic matters were necessary, it would indisputably be Jean-Jacques Rousseau," writes Michel Onfray. "Should we be surprised to read a proper critique of gastronomy by a philosopher like this? Certainly not. The entire work is proof of its author's fundamental incapacity for any kind of cheerful learning, including in the area of food."[41]

Severe, but so very just. "It is only the French," fulminates Jean-Jacques in *Emile*, "who don't know how to eat, since they need so special an art to produce edible dishes for them."[42] For him, the ideal meal is a vegetarian tea party beside a stream, made up of dairy products, eggs, herbs, dark bread, and fresh young wine.[43] We are reminded of Marie Antoinette and her hamlet, but this is not a matter of simple diversion. Eating is a serious kind of communion with the wild, with "nature" and with peasant labor in its primitive state. All cultural and especially hedonistic embellishments to food were treason against it and damaging to the one ingesting it. At the end of the twentieth century, this became one of the cultural components of the "*nouvelle cuisine*" phenomenon, along with many other, fortunately less radical ones! Rousseau goes even further; he quite simply does away with taste. With regard to Julie, he writes, "Her sense of taste has hardly been used; she never needs to revive it with excesses, and I often see her savoring with delight a child's treat that would be tasteless to all others."[44]

For the Genevan, as for certain thinkers of the "Enlightenment," luxury is also responsible for creating the poverty all around it:

> We must have juice in our kitchens; that is why so many sick people lack broth. We must have liqueurs on our tables; that is way the peasant drinks only water. We must have powder on our wigs; that is why so many among the poor have no bread.[45]

It is so easy to purchase a clean conscience by drinking milk! A naive, strange, and finally dangerous illusion, a modern version of which we find again today in certain moralizing political discourse or in the newspapers and God-fearing sermons at Christmastime. As if depriving oneself of truffles and foie gras could be of some help to Sahelian peasants! They forget that the planet's poorest inhabitants have always feasted generously and joyously when the opportunity has presented itself, and that they will sacrifice their meager wealth, killing their last sheep or chicken, for a stranger's visit.

The French Huguenots are very close to their famous fellow Genevan. Thus, around 1780, Bertin describes the Saintonge where they are so numerous:[46]

> Here, nothing speaks to the imagination. Everything is sad, wild, inanimate. I especially pity the gourmands on this route: they can hardly claim to encounter here
>
> *Those good patés, those Angoulême truffles,*
> *Those Tours fruits, that lovely Grois wine*
> *Matured farther away, and the flattering cream*
> *That working girls around Blois*
> *Make froth up lightly under fingers*
> *So white they slander the milk itself.*
>
> Bad food and bad roads, that is the canton's slogan.

As with Voltaire, Bertin may be exaggerating a bit, as is true of all popular discourse concerning the customs of the French Protestant minority. But, as the saying goes, you only lend money to the rich. In her biography of Elisée Reclus, the son of an austere Methodist pastor, Hélène Sarrazin relates a very significant anecdote:

> One lovely day, a well-intentioned parishioner brought Madame Reclus a goose, a beautiful goose. The goose was roasted, it arrived all golden brown to the table, and the children's mouths were watering with happiness when the pastor entered. Before saying grace, he demanded, "Wife, what is this?" "A goose that Madame Unetelle has offered us." "Take it to someone poorer than you!" And the goose disappeared from the table.[47]

Thus it was completely natural for the French Protestants to wage war against alcoholism during the time of the industrial revolution. They were very active in temperance societies, and the first abstinence society, "The French Blue Cross," was created by a Pastor Bianquis in 1890.[48] They followed the example of their Scandinavian counterparts. From the mid-nineteenth century, the latter had succeeded in reducing the consumption of alcohol, limiting the number and the business hours of drinking establishments, and forbidding them to provide credit and . . . places to sit down. That was how Sweden lost its place as the country with the highest alcohol consumption.[49] Karen Blixen's lovely short story, *Babette's Feast*,[50] a Scandinavian homage to French *haute cuisine*, describes the alarmed expressions of the members of a small Protestant sect finding themselves forced to sample fine French wines and bite into quail stuffed with foie gras. All's well that ends well, and everyone leaves transfigured by the experience. . . .

We will not conclude by listing similar examples showing Protestants to be indifferent or hostile to eating well, from Rousseau obsessed with so-called nature to Sartre compulsively consuming heavy, fatty foods, tobacco, medications, and alcohol without pleasure.[51] In contrast to Stephen Mennell and a few others who deny the Reformation's aversion to gastronomy and accuse those who adopt such a view of Weberian simplism, there are many Protestants today who admit to it with good humor and sometimes a touch of regret. Let us cite Patricia Wells, the well-known American food columnist,[52] or the Canadian Arthur Sager, who writes:

> It cannot be denied that most British feel a bit sinful when food is too good, and for this reason they beg for divine indulgence. For them, "gourmand" and "gourmet" are only wicked French words, and nobody in the United Kingdom has ever found an equivalent expression for "bon appétit." They have never even imagined such an idea.[53]

And again, let us quote that dynamic statesman, Remy Sautter, a minister's son, who avoids social events and dinners and explains why, a smile playing at the corner of his mouth: "That must be my Protestant side."[54]

No doubt we must also consider the geography of restaurants, with exceptions, as related to the religious geography. For a long time, Marseilles, Bordeaux, Montpellier, Nîmes, Mulhouse, and Montbéliard had no really good restaurants. Now those were the places the great Protestant middle class was dominant or influential in the nineteenth century, when *haute cuisine* was developing everywhere else. Today, everything has changed, but only because a restaurant is not just a workshop for artistic creation and pleasure; it is also a place where business is conducted. To conduct it successfully, you can make the effort to eat ortolans.

In demonstrating the Reformation's repressive role with regard to gastronomy, we are only forcing a door already long open, one that only a few lovers of paradox would like to see shut again. Todd's idea has yet to be explored,[55] according to which a direct link exists between Protestantism and the dynastic family, the breeding ground for that religious pessimism simultaneously encouraging feverish mental and physical activity and thus "success" but also a renunciation of pleasure.

The Catholic Reformation, or With Closed Eyes

It would be too easy, however, to oppose to an austere and anorexic Reformation Europe a Counter-Reformation Europe uniformly joyous and relaxed at the table. Locally and at certain times, it also chose the narrow path, in keeping with the council of Trente: "The body must be trained not only by fasts, and especially by those the Church prescribes, but also by vigils, holy pilgrimages, and other mortifications," reads the catechism of Trente completed by the somber Saint Charles Borromée in 1566.[56]

In Spain, a mystical and solemn expression of the religion flourished, headed entirely in this direction. In his *Guide for Sinners*, published in 1555, translated into every language, and reissued frequently until the eighteenth century, the Dominican Louis of Granada denounces the senses, taste in particular:

> Among all our bodily senses, there are none more contemptible than those of taste and touch: because all the animals of the world, as imperfect as they may be, make

> use of these two senses, even though many are deprived of the other three, which are sight, smell, and hearing: and thus, as these two senses are the most vile and the most material of all, so are all the pleasures assigned to them.[57]

The renunciation advocated by Saint Theresa of Avila is directly related to that of the Desert Fathers: "The unavoidable necessity of eating and sleeping and so many other of life's constraints, must they not also make us aware of our misery and lead to our desire to go a place that will set us free?"[58] At this time, Spain was governed by a monarch who lived as an ascetic in a convent-monastery, its plan reminiscent of the grill on which Saint Laurence was roasted alive. We have to admit that the climate was not propitious for the development of fine court cooking exciting a palace full of courtesans and teasing their sensual imaginations. That does not keep the Spanish people from being less attached to observing Lent than most Europeans, first of all because freshwater fish are rare there, and especially because of the "bull of the Crusade," known as the Lepante indulgence, which authorized the faithful, in return for a fee, to eat butter, lard, and cheese.[59] It is true that this is nothing new, and if the Rouen cathedral is adorned with a "tower of butter," it is very much for the same reason.

In France, a whole segment of Church men and high society were attracted to an analogous model, the Jansenist doctrine. For the Jansenists, the world is contemptible and the senses condemned. We can read in *Hope for Divine Love* (1625): "To hear, to speak, to taste, to touch or manipulate or feel no matter how"[60] is suspect as soon as one finds "pleasure and delight" there. *Urania Victrix* ("The battles of the Christian soul") is a long and extraordinary poem in Latin verse composed between 1657 and 1663 by the Alsatian Jesuit Jacob Balde. Along with

Michel Serres's recent attempt,[61] it is one of the rare literary and philosophical works on the five senses. In this elegy, he presents the senses as admirers courting the soul, who rejects them in order to remain faithful to Christ. Uranie (the soul) refuses the advances of Rumpold the cook, who tries to tempt her with fine foods:

> Save your dishes: I am not at all a woman for dishes;
> Such ordinary food betrays a venal soul.
> Esau sold his birthright for vile lentils,

More vile himself, the madman! What are you doing, impudent glutton?

> The delicacies and tidbits you present me, I spit on
> Above; I am satisfied by a heavenly food.
> It is not to eat that I live, but I eat, Rumpold
> Caracalla, to stay alive. Life is for living, not eating.
> Add this: your pleasure is brief and not real;
> as it lacks a solid duration, it evaporates.
> Every wise man always disdains it and considers it below
> Him, to whom virtue is precious.[62]

We find the same tendency in Pascal, with less of that lyric excess:

> Do not pity me in the least . . . disease is the natural state of Christians, because there we are as we should always be, that is, in the midst of suffering and ills, deprived of all earthly goods and sensual pleasures, exempt from passions, free of ambition and greed, and continually awaiting death.[63]

But some trace of the Gallo-Roman tradition also makes him say, "Too much and too little wine; do not give it to him, he cannot find the truth; give him too much of it, all the same."[64]

From the middle of the eighteenth century and especially after the *Unigenitus* bull (1713), the progress of Jansenism in France was checked, just as Catharism and the Reformation were. There are undeniable political reasons for this, but there is also French culture's reluctance to adopt excessively austere models.

For all that, the roots of Jansenism, or at least of its moral aspects, were not eradicated; shoots periodically appear. Persecuted by the Republic at the beginning of this century, the Church sought its salvation in defending such principles. In its advice to devout young soldiers dating from 1913, we can read, for example:

> And there you are at the table. Eat simply according to your appetite. Above all, do not turn your nose up at the food; you will see plenty of others doing that. Believe me, a good soldier must eat "everyday fare," and all that is given him, like all the others. I do not think much of those young whippersnappers who look disdainful and go off to eat in the canteen or in town. . . . Eat and drink moderately and simply. The one who prefers water, milk, and fruit to alcohol fortifies his health and increases his capacity for work and happiness.[65]

You'd think this was Rousseau! The same language was used by clergy during World War II. It is true that restrictions did not allow for excess and the French had to be consoled. . . . But there are methods, and then there are methods. . . . In *Le Caporal épinglé* (*The Pinned Corporal*), Jacques Perret describes the pleasure he felt eating powdered sugar during this time, when he was caught in a perilous position under a train in the course of an escape. It is an optimistic vision of misfortune. Here are the castrating words of a good clergyman: "The means to be taken in order to have a strong body: 1) A healthy and abundant (but not meticulous) diet. A little meat, many fruits and vegetables."[66]

Those pious, restrained tea parties focused around some edifying conversation, still held today in certain Christian communities, exist henceforth as much among Catholics as Protestants. Third-Worldism has united many of them, and when one believes in that, there is no question of eating well. A study must be done of the whole parallel movement for purifying the flesh that brought mainstream Protestantism and French Catholicism together in the twentieth century. Freud covered the same ground, arriving at the open bed, the clean table, and death to the unconscious transference of flesh onto food. Whereas, since the sixteenth century, the French Catholic ethic was rather the opposite: the half-closed bed and guilt (the transgression only made it more enjoyable), a table well supplied and celebratory, no real restraint. As Robert Sauzet has shown,[67] during the Renaissance and in modern times, the French clergy has shown itself to be willingly adept at "frank sensual pleasure . . . perhaps as compensation for other more complete denials."

Nothing is too good for God. That is the moral behind the Bernis cardinal's famous practice of only celebrating his mass with a fine Meaursault, so as not to make the Lord grimace at communion time. "A good cake stolen remains a good cake," "You can be on a diet and still look at the menu," etc.: that is how today's ecclesiastics good-naturedly express the Catholic conception of the sins of sensuality,[68] too easily labeled hypocritical even though it is drawn from the Gospel and the whole ancient interpretive tradition.

If we only consider gourmandism, intemperance, and drunkenness, we will notice that at the height of the Counter-Reformation, these sins were only addressed in 4 percent of the sermons preached and published by 11 preachers in the seventeenth and eighteenth centuries, while lust was in 17.5 percent, greed in 16.8 percent, envy and slander in 10.6 percent.[69] Much perversion would have to be exercised for this sin, however common in France, to become mortal. As a "weakness," as any interest in the good things in life was then called, it was not at all reprehensible. In 1600, in *La Somme des péchés et remèdes d'iceux* (*The Survey of Sins and Their Remedies*),[70] J. Benedicti only considers the sin of gourmandism mortal if it is committed "to the detriment of oneself or one's fellow man" and especially if "the gourmand does not pay his debts and lets his family die of hunger."

And Saint François de Sales, for whom "it is necessary to take care of the body in order for the soul to be happy there," wrote that the devout person must "eat, not simply to maintain life, but to maintain the mutual conversation and condescension that we must have for one another. It is an absolutely just and honest thing."[71] As we can see, the amiable Genevan bishop *in partibus* was miles away from the thinking of the Calvinists among whom he worked as a missionary. He was the one who, after giving a Lenten sermon in Annecy, preferred to be paid with a cask of Seysell wine rather than a hundred gold pieces. We can imagine that the mortifications for the aforementioned Lent must have been quickly forgotten! These are the pious attitudes of François de Sales's disciples that Brillat-Savarin, a citizen of Belley and thus within this sphere of influence, analyzed so skillfully two centuries later:

> It is among those things that are unequivocally damned, and never to be allowed, like dancing, shows, games, and

> other similar pastimes. While these are loathed, along with those who practice them, the gourmand presents himself and slips by with a completely theological face.[72]

How could the Counter-Reformation have engendered some other philosophy? Emmanuel Todd recalls that it began within an optimistic Europe, long devoted to the rules of the egalitarian nuclear family. The father could not disinherit his children; God could not damn his creatures if they respected the law and had recourse to his mercy after sinning, with the condition that contrition intervened at least a second before the crime. From then on, even if you did not know the day or the hour of your death, you could make an effort and take advantage of the joys of existence rather than floundering about in the mires of the vale of tears. You could—and in fact, you were supposed to—express the pleasure of living in architecture, sculpture, music, and of course, cooking. Nothing was too beautiful for celebrating the overabundance of grace: the cherubs streaming with gold tumbling from the clouds overhanging the altars; in beatific triumph they rivaled the motets in twelve voices, fireworks, ribboned costumes, and complex recipes. Here, the dreams of the Prince were fully blessed by the Church.

An entire work would not be enough to compile all the supporting evidence. One of the most eloquent nineteenth-century testimonies is the message contained in the *Lettres de mon Moulin* (*Letters from My Mill*), appearing in 1869. After a cool reception, Daudet's short stories experienced great success, for their style first of all but also for the pleasant moral atmosphere they evoke, especially with regard to food. Dom Balaguère, the chaplain employed by the lords of Trinquelage, celebrates his three low Christmas masses in the gourmand's pure state of sin: "Two turkeys stuffed with truffles, Garrigou? . . . Let us hurry, let us hurry. . . . The sooner we're finished, the sooner we'll be at the table. . . . O delight! There's the immense table completely loaded and gleaming." Daudet, fine connoisseur of the doctrine, plunges him first "into eternal damnation," and then, after the attack that kills him "without having had even the time to repent," he saves him from hell and delivers him to purgatory: " 'Withdraw from my sight, bad Christian!' said the sovereign Judge our master to him. 'Your fault is big enough to erase a whole life of virtue. . . . Ah! You have stolen a night's mass from me. . . . Very well, you will pay me three hundred of them in its place.' "

No contradiction in this beautiful story, but on the contrary, a smiling restitution of what is most profound and permanent in the Catholic moral code in France. Jesuitism, we might call the Prémontré abbot's solution for authorizing Father Gaucher's alcoholism in order to maintain the revenues of the monastery and the morale of the monks; simple tolerance, in reality, for a minor sin is capable of engendering so many benefits. A right can be born from a wrong; no idea is more Christian: blessed original sin that earned humanity the Incarnation of the Son of God!

In the first half of the twentieth century, if they were neo-Jansenist in some of their attitudes, the French clergy remained mostly inclined toward leniency when it came to gourmandism. We can see how far they had come since the time of the Church Fathers by reading the commentaries on Saint Benoît's rule written by Father Paul Delatter in 1919 from the influential abbey of Solesmes. Evoking the storeroom keeper, he is not shy in expressing his reservations about Saint Benoît himself, who wanted him to have very austere habits:

> Perhaps there was special occasion for this advice in a time when barbarian habits led to excess; today we would

> more willingly advise the abbot to take on a storeroom keeper who eats and drinks! In reality, it would be dangerous to trust the community's food service . . . to an ascetic, to a monk who lives very cheaply and remains below the average everyday measure.[73]

As surprising as it may seem within an order that has taken itself so seriously and has so often reprimanded its contemporaries over the decades, there are two Dominicans competing in eloquence, these last few years, when it comes to glorifying the pleasures of eating well. Father Maurice Lelong delights—and not without malicious intent—in turning pleasant works to the glory of earthly sustenance: bread, wine, cheese, sausage, etc.[74] Father Serge Bonnet too, in providing, among other things, a mouth-watering preface to the new edition of Auricost de Lazarque.[75] For authority he calls upon Abbot Migne, the well-known publisher of Greek and Latin Patrologies, who wrote in 1848, "Gourmandism indicates a willing resignation to the orders of the Creator who, having commanded us to eat in order to live, invites us to do so through appetite, sustains us through taste, and rewards us through pleasure."[76] And Serge Bonnet continues with a rare eulogy to gluttony:

> The brief trouble that follows excessive eating must not make us forget that the four nails used to crucify Jesus Christ are named: hate, pride, slander, and jealousy. Beside these abominable sins, the delightful sins . . . among which we can include the lapses of gourmandism, are hardly anything. Gourmandism becomes a sin when it leads the gourmand to stuff his digestive organs so much that he becomes incapable of communion with his fellow man.

It is not surprising that this good-natured appreciation of good eating in a Christian spirit should remain—and until very recently—more in evidence among rural Catholics (practicing and "cultural") than among urbanites, more easily drawn to the political and social ideas of intellectuals. The Cauchois cleric, Bernard Alexandre, who ate no fat in his entire life, echoes this in *Le Horsain*, slightly bitter because he has let himself be a bit won over by the platitudes of the time, but with an eye moist with affection for his parishioners all the same.[77] The account of a pilgrimage to Lisieux ending in a binge is destined to become a classic. One of his spiritual advisors, moreover, had shown him the relaxed way of the Gospel during a prolonged stay at the sanitarium: "What you must admit first of all is that the best cure for your ills is your willingness to live happily. . . . Optimism is a duty. God wants us to be happy and as soon as possible."[78]

Certainly the most beautiful Christian eulogy to gastronomy comes from the *Plaidoyer pour le corps* (*In Defense of the Body*), published in the midst of the war by V. Poucel:

> To eat blindly, without knowing what you are doing, is, first of all, to profane a holy thing; next, it is to stop the growth of a life that stems from the earth to yield in goodness. It will spread through the body without reaching those obstructed avenues of the soul. . . . There is a state of mind at meals, a clear-sightedness, from which nobility arises: then we understand where life originates and where it is going. The loss of that essential faith, almost a kind of intelligence, is a fatal sign of mindlessness. . . . At that table where [the guests] are about to sit down, a noble rite is about to take place, creating a kinship between blood brothers and strangers, through the living communion of matter itself. The veins of our ancestor, Earth,

> will open and distribute into various reunited bodies a more homogeneous blood. . . . Eat! Drink! Thus gain access to the perceptible forms of Divine Will![79]

As we can see, the old Gallic paganism, so close to animism, always gets along well with Christian monotheism, and the most inspired of today's great cooks will find in these poetic lines one of the forces behind their art, one rarely emphasized by the critic.

Thus, to untangle the web of rules and attitudes European Christians have developed with regard to food, especially much sought-after food, is no easy thing. We can arrive at a hypothesis but not at a peremptory and definitive conclusion. The French Catholic world, but also the Italian Catholic world, heir to the apostolic seat, has never consistently curbed man's "natural" and eternal inclination to eat and drink as well as possible. Invoking Protestantism for the other regions is probably justified, but we must refer back to Emmanuel Todd's explanations for the grounds for this geography. There may also be another factor: northern Europe was only slightly if at all Romanized and only gained access to the Roman cultural heritage, in part culinary, with its conversion to Christianity. Often this was recent, only dating back to the thirteenth century, as in Finland, for example. This handicap is not permanent, but time will be needed to make up for it.

Chapter Three

Governing at the Table: Birth of a Model

A CULTURAL TRADITION OF SOCIABLE reveling and celebration at the table, not fundamentally at odds with the religious moral code even if tempered by it: that is the French context for the birth of *haute cuisine*. But, as already mentioned, such an explanation is insufficient, because that tradition is found in Italy as well, a country where, from early on, good food has been greatly appreciated by the whole society, with even fewer exceptions than in France.

Moreover, looking closely, there is no one unified great Italian cuisine but many flavorful regional cuisines, created from local or imported products, prepared with more or less refinement, in the country style or in the style of the closest town (*alla bolognese*, *alla milanese*, *alla fiorentina*, etc.). Consider a few glories of Florentine cooking: flavorful *bistecca* right out of a baker's oven, simply seasoned, before baking, with coarse salt and pepper; brochettes of little birds roasted with sage; or large melting beans trickled with green, fruity olive oil. Nothing stirs the gourmet's imagination more than the sincerity of these dishes that resonate with the surrounding landscape and Tuscan elegance.

We find this regional model again throughout Europe and the world. Diversifying with agricultural development, increased financial resources of the inhabitants, and strengthening cultural identities, these rural cuisines, ancient as they may be, are most often a matter of family heritage. Recipes involving numerous variations are transmitted from mother to daughter or daughter-in-law, even if they are sometimes co-opted by professional cooks. Only the preparation of a few rare dishes, roast meats for example, is reserved for men, which perpetuates a very ancient, perhaps even Neolithic, tradition. Paella, *tagine*, cassoulet, *potée*, sauerkraut, daube, carbonnade, moussaka, *tie-bou-diène*, chili con carne, chop suey, curry, sushi, and a thousand other dishes throughout the world are rooted in one rural region but open to the transfusion of exotic ingredients assimilated little by little even to the point of replacing the older ones. That is the case, let us recall, with the tomato and the long bean, which phased out the cabbage and the broad bean in Mediterranean countries. Regional Italian cuisines are comparable to the cuisines of Perigord, Auvergne, Normandy, or Alsace. Local agriculture combines with influences from the city or introduced by way of trade routes.

Today, to eat foie gras, sauerkraut, Muenster cheese, and Gewurztraminer marc sorbet at the Kammerzell house of Strasbourg is to participate simultaneously in Jewish expertise with regard to raising geese; the oldest Germanic traditions for preparing sour cabbage; the conquest of America and the potato accompanying it; the Vosges mountain life where cheese was almost the only thing to sell, except for wood; seventeenth-century dietary habits with the caraway accompanying the

Muenster,[1] and Mediterranean traditions of conserving snow ("sorbet" comes from the Arabic *charbât*), transmitted to northern countries via Italy. As for the Alsatian wine, it is a Roman legacy to the Rhenish regions. And nevertheless, to eat at the foot of the Strasbourg cathedral gives the "inland French" the impression of communing with a culture as ancient as it is autonomous, that is, strictly local. A false impression, as everywhere else! Our epoch needs the reassuring belief in a permanent heritage as the only stable value. It is difficult to condemn, because there are good reasons for it, but we thus deprive ourselves of a veritable fireworks of cultural exchanges and access to other, deeper kinds of security.

The City, Crucible for Eating Well

The most elaborate version of this model is, of course, urban. Complex dishes highlighting choice products can only develop where a well-stocked market exists but also where there is money and leisure, as well as a culture that allows fantasies of luxury and sensual pleasure to flourish. Let us add to these conditions the power and the more or less ostentatious desire for outward display. The storyteller Noël du Fail maintains that in the sixteenth century, "In the towns, expenditures for clothes as well as for feasts and games are excessive."[2] The environment of independent artists, well-to-do merchants, lawyers, city officials, and other categories of urbanites benefiting from regular and substantial income is very favorable for the development of fine cooking when, at the same time, the moral code offers no opposition to it.

We can witness this phenomenon, as old as urbanization, with Babylon, Thebes, Rome, Carthage, Byzantium, Granada, Mexico, Peking, and Kyoto. We know of the extreme refinement—some would say decadence and pretension—of the banquets served in imperial Rome and in the vacation towns of southern Italy, despite the sumptuary laws. Marco Polo reported a fascination for eating well that reigned in thirteenth-century Hangchou, the capital of the southern Sung, on the eve of the invasion by Kubla Khan. "The time and thus the memory was permeated with impressions of food," writes Michael Freeman on the subject of this city where everything came down to the table, including philosophers' and historians' discourse.[3]

The great European cities of the Middle Ages, whether they were principalities or largely independent, all allowed the gastronomic spark to shine forth and the great wines to be born in those surrounding areas where the climate permitted it. Florence, Venice, Genoa, Bruges, and a few others were pioneers, perhaps because the gourmands, that is, the middle class, resided there on a permanent basis, whereas elsewhere in Europe the higher-ranking aristocrats were seminomadic.

In France, outside of Paris, one of the most renowned gourmet cities has always been Lyons. The market fairs, the artisans, and the silk merchants solicited from the surrounding areas high-quality products and recipes to match. This phenomenon goes back at least to the sixteenth century, as Erasmus, so difficult to satisfy at the table, testifies:

> One is not treated better at home than in a Lyons inn. The mother of the family arrives first to greet you, wishing you good cheer and hoping what you will be pleased by what you are served. The table is truly sumptuous, and I am astonished that they can serve their guests at such a low price.[4]

Berchoux confirms the excellence of Lyonnaise cooking under the Empire:

> *Would you like to succeed in the art I profess?*
> *Get a nice castle in Auvergne or Bresse,*
> *Or near those charming places from which Lyons sees pass*
> *Two rivers deep in love and all ready to embrace.*
> *You will procure for yourself, under that sky so favorable,*
> *All that serves to sweeten the pleasures of the table.*[5]

And Brillat-Savarin, a man of Bugey, a region under Lyonnaise influence, goes a step further:

> Lyons is a city for eating well; its location makes for an equally accessible and abundant supply of Bordeaux wines, Ermitage wines, and Burgundy wines; the game from the neighboring hillsides is excellent; the world's best fish are caught in the Geneva and Bourget lakes; and devotees go ecstatic at the sight of Bresse pullets, for which this city serves as warehouse.[6]

These last words make the gastronomic role of the city clear: it elicits premium products from the surrounding countryside and draws them to its markets where they find buyers, even if their prices are high. Thus, the Lyonnaise *quenelle* calls for pike raised in the Dombes ponds and the soft part of lower Dauphinois wheat bread, and for its *sauce Nantua*, crayfish from Bugey, cream from Bresse, and white wine from Mâcon or Montagnieu.

Three quarters of a century later, the scene is further enhanced. Paul de Courselles and Sixte Delorme do not yet suspect that Bocuse and Chapel will bring the planet's best products to their establishments but can already trace a zone of attraction, its radius more than a hundred kilometers long:

> Imagine the quantity and diversity of goods that can reach Lyons by waterways and railways. . . . Those Burgundy wines . . . and those Mâcons and Beaujolais and Côtes-du-Rhônes, the most full-bodied, the most generous; and the fat poultry and plump quadrupeds, with their pink snouts, their wiggly tails, that our glorious butcher shops award the prize; and the *becs-fins* from our vineyards, and the ortolans from the blackberry bushes, and the quail from Valbonne, and the woodcocks from the Bresse woods, and the chamois from the Dauphinois Alps, and the trout from Albarine and the *féra* from Léman, and the excellent fruits that you will see tomorrow, in heaps, at the market on Saint-Antoine quay, and the cheeses from Mont-Dore, Gex, Sassenage, Saint-Marcellin.[7]

An excellent illustration of the role cities play is provided by the geography of cheeses.[8] Most of them—they say as many kinds exist as there are days in the year; many more, in fact—have long been produced strictly for local and peasant consumption. "Cheese," writes Claude Thouvenot with regard to the Lorraine, is "too ordinary in everyday life. One hesitates a long time over offering it for a holiday meal."[9] Official gastronomy had even accepted this stance, since at Elysée, in De Gaulle's time, cheese was not mentioned on the menu, even when it was served.[10] That had not always been the case, since, during antiquity and then afterward beginning from the twelfth century, certain cheeses were prized enough by the aristocracy or the cities' bourgeoisie to be imported and sold at high prices. As was true for wines, the cities played the role of magnet with regard to an extraordinarily far-flung map of cheeses. And also, as with the wine-making model, abbeys had a part in the emergence of quality cheeses. Thus, in the fourteenth century, cheese from the abbey of Maroilles, in Thiérache, was sold in towns in Flanders and Champagne, and in Paris.[11] As early as the Middle Ages, *géromé* from the Vosges, Brie, Roquefort, and *comté* rose from anonymity and were appreciated in towns both near and far from the areas of their origin. Even if the flavor of cheeses has probably greatly evolved during the modern period in step with technical improvements, their division into fresh, soft, or hard cheeses dates back to the Middle Ages. In this, it is a matter of zoning according to the theory of Von Thünen, that is, privileging the distance from the market,[12] the perishable and hard-to-transport cheeses being produced right outside the towns and the hard cheeses, pressed cheeses (raw or cooked), or veined cheeses being produced in zones far from urban centers, especially in the mountains (see map 1). The hierarchy of sizes is the same: they are proportional to the distance from the markets for urban consumption, with the notable exception of Brie. Many mountain cheeses, produced in the high mountain or summer pastures, were sold only in the fall, when the herds went back down to the valleys. During the summer, the milk from the feudal domain's whole herd or from all the animals in a village was collected together each day, as is still done in the cheese dairies of the Jura. Because of the volume processed and the need to preserve it, the cheese was of a very large size.

The example of Auvergne cheeses in the eighteenth century is indicative of the roles played by the city and transportation routes in the quality of food production.[13] Until that period, these cheeses had no reputation in Paris and could find buyers only in Provence and Languedoc, and only with difficulty there, because of their mediocrity. Thus, in 1765, the subdelegate of Aurillac wrote, "If the great road from Aurillac to Figeac through Maurs was completed, the farmers would load

THE PRINCIPAL TRADITIONAL FRENCH CHEESES

up with cheeses for Quercy, Toulouse, and Bordeaux." Lacking a good road, they could only improve the quality of their products. Even Roquefort reached Paris and Rome; why not the various *fourmes*? It was on this task that many of the province's intendants and subdelegates set themselves to work. In 1733, Trudaine, Auvergne's intendant, had recruited a family of Dutch cowherds whom he sent to the subdelegate of Mauriac. "I have no advice to give you," he wrote, "except to provide them with everything they need to make cheese as they do in their country and . . . to do everything within your power to convince them to stay in the country." But the Dutch barely succeeded in their enterprise and left the area a few months later. Trudaine then tried to bring in some Swiss cowherds. A model cheese dairy was built for their benefit in the middle of which sat enthroned a copper cauldron. Aurillac's subdelegate wrote in 1734, "The Swiss are succeeding wonderfully; the cheeses really fill out and put on weight like those of Gryer."[14] But in the high country, foreigners appointed to give lessons are not looked upon kindly. Various malicious rumors explain why, in 1739, the Swiss left again for home. We must believe, nonetheless, that these attempts bore fruit, since in the early nineteenth century, Auvergne cheeses reached northern France[15] and since Cantal sits nobly enthroned, unscathed there in the heat and stench of the cheese stall described by Zola in *Le Ventre de Paris*.[16]

If further proof were needed, one last example will show how the urban gourmand can dictate to the farmers by requiring of them, via the cook, the *ne plus ultra*. Interestingly, this is drawn from Escoffier's *Memoirs*; he claims, moreover, that France is, quite naturally, the Land of Milk and Honey.[17] This testimony's precision makes it a potential classic, worth quoting in full.

When the old baron of Rothschild came to dine at the Grand Hotel in Monte Carlo, he wanted none but "green" asparagus. To satisfy him, the fattest were chosen from among the bunches of asparagus tips. I then noticed, at the Savoy in London, that the English preferred green asparagus to white. Thus, I had shipped to me from France some little bundles of fat tips. They were such a success that the demand became greater than the supply, and from one day to the next, the price of these bundles doubled. Faced with the producer's demands, I began to look for a competitor, to curb continual price increases. One Sunday morning, I went to a café in Mérindol, a village near Lauris in the Vaucluse, to meet with the principal asparagus growers there. I said to them, "Sirs, you produce absolutely beautiful asparagus, but growing it is a lot of work, and you do not reap the benefits commensurate with your efforts. I live in London, where I am in charge of the kitchens for a large hotel. And the English prefer green asparagus. Would you be disposed toward taking an interest in cultivating this crop? I can guarantee you large profits." A bit surprised, all these good gentlemen responded that producing green asparagus would require them to change their whole system, and they did not see how that was possible. Than a young man about twenty years old spoke up: "Why not? Alongside our large asparagus, we have a lot of little ones that we can only get rid of at ridiculous prices. Let's let them grow out of the soil, and the part that gets light will become green." Everyone understood the significance of this idea, and from that day on, Lauris sent green asparagus to England! Its success greatly surpassed my expectations. Only Lauris's green asparagus are now found in

> London. The big white asparagus of the past have become green. I must say I have never had the honor of receiving a bunch of asparagus from a producer. Nevertheless, my advice surely made some of them their fortunes.[18]

"Il n'est bon bec que de Paris"

We know that François Villon's lovely verse[19] applies only to the pretty little faces and chatter of Parisians, but the gourmands' misinterpretation of its meaning and their new use for it are not totally absurd, since the gastronomic reputation of Paris is unbroken and very old. It is important to understand the genesis of this phenomenon, because French *haute cuisine* is, first and foremost, a Parisian phenomenon.

In the Middle Ages and the Renaissance, Paris, like all major cities where much money circulates, allowed gourmandism to be practiced easily. Two books written in the fourteenth century, one in the circles of the court, one in bourgeois circles, attest to the refinement Parisian cooking had attained as early as this period. *Le Viandier*, attributed to Guillaume Tirel, called Taillevent, the first chef for Charles VI, was compiled throughout the fourteenth century, and *Le Ménagier de Paris* was written about 1392 by an old husband worried about teaching good principles to his young wife.[20] Parisian cuisine of the time easily rivaled that of Italian cities, London, Dijon, or Bruges. The feasts served there on important occasions consisted of a profusion of dishes, especially meat dishes (venison as well as butcher's meat), accompanied by tart sauces, seasoned with innumerable spices, many of which have disappeared from our tables. Beyond their antiseptic and digestive qualities with regard to meat conserved under not very hygienic conditions, spices were, above all, the outward sign of wealth and power.

For the sixteenth century (1577) we have at our disposal a brief but remarkable testimony on the quality of Parisian eating, among the wealthy as well as more modest urbanites. It is all the more reliable and revealing since it does not come from a witness from the country, a little village, or a "barbaric" land but from an Italian, no less than the Venetian ambassador to the king of France, Jérôme Lippomano. His surprise leads us to think that Paris was somewhat of an exceptional city from the perspective that concerns us, which may have already been the case prior to that time (though we have no proof).

> Pork is the usual food of the poor people, but only those who are truly poor. Every worker, every merchant, no matter how pinched, wants to eat mutton, venison, and partridge on days with meat just as the rich do; and on days with no meat, the salmon, cod, and salt herring that are brought from Holland and the northern islands in great number. Paris stores are packed with them. They also eat fresh butter and dairy products. Vegetables are abundant there, especially white and green peas. . . . Paris has plenty of everything you could desire. Goods from every country pour into it; provisions arrive there on the Seine from Picardie, Auvergne, Burgundy, Champagne, and Normandy. Also, although the population is enormous, there is nothing lacking there. Everything seems to fall from the sky. However, the price of food is a bit high there, actually, because the French spend money on nothing so willingly as on eating and on making what they call "good cheer." That is why butchers, meat merchants, roast meat sellers, retailers, pastry bakers, and keepers of inns and taverns are

found in such quantity that it is truly chaos. There is not a street, no matter how unremarkable, that doesn't play its part. Would you like to buy animals at the market, or even meat? You can do so, at any hour, in any location. Would you like your supplies all prepared, cooked, or raw? In less than an hour, the roast meat sellers and the pastry bakers can arrange a dinner or a supper for you, serving ten, serving twenty, serving a hundred people. The roast meat seller gives you the meat; the pastry baker gives you the pâtés, the pies, the entrées, the desserts; the cook gives you the aspics, the sauces, the ragoûts. This art is so advanced in Paris that there are innkeepers who will have you to eat there, at any cost, for a penny, for a crown, for four, for ten, for even twenty per person if you wish. But for twenty crowns, they will give you, I hope, the manna in the soup, or roasted phoenix; all, finally, that is most precious in the world. The princes and the king go there sometimes.[21]

The law of the food profession's supply and the gourmands' demand already fully applied. Among the latter was the king himself, who was not averse to eating out sometimes. Paris wove close ties with northern France; its network would never stop extending, just like its reputation in Europe, which continues to grow and be embellished to this day. The fact that today some of the best Belgian, German, and Swiss restaurant owners have their raw materials delivered from Rungis is only one result of this whole process.

Before returning to the crucial sixteenth century, let us mention gourmand Paris at the beginning of the nineteenth century. In gastronomic matters, the 1790s were not at all revolutionary, and Europe's best products still flowed into that city. Grimod de La Reynière notes:

> It is undeniably the place in the universe where the finest food is made, and the only one capable of providing excellent cooks to all the civilized nations of the world. Although Paris by itself produces nothing, because not a single grain of wheat is grown there, not a single lamb is raised, not a single cauliflower harvested, it is a center where everything finally ends up from all the corners of the earth, because it is the place where the respective qualities of everything useful to human nourishment are best appreciated, and where they know best how to make the most of these for the benefit of our senses.[22]

And he rejoices at the fruits available at the Halle market: "You see strawberries there in the month of January, grapes at Easter, and pineapples all year round. The sun's course is reversed, the seasons are mixed up, and the two hemispheres merge to add one dish more to the brilliant desserts of our modern Luculluses."[23]

As for Brillat-Savarin—even though he greatly admires Lyons—"a meal such as can be had in Paris is an entirely cosmopolitan one in which each part of the world appears through its products."[24] Evoking the ideal table of a certain Monsieur de Borose, a marvelous gourmet in his opinion, he exclaims, "At all times his table presented the best the season could offer, either its most rare or its earliest." Reading Grimod and Brillat-Savarin reveals how truly well stocked Paris was with national and international products (see map 2). That Parisian specialty *par excellence*, ham pâté, entirely owes its exquisite taste at M. Leblanc's, rue de la Harpe, to the 1,800 Bayonne hams he stores each year in April all over his house in order to make it.[25] In February, the mail coaches harbor as many letters as truffled turkeys, if we are to believe Grimod, "embalming all dispatches

HOW PARIS WAS SUPPLIED GASTRONOMICALLY IN THE EARLY NINETEENTH CENTURY

According to Grimod de La Reyniére and Brillat-Savarin

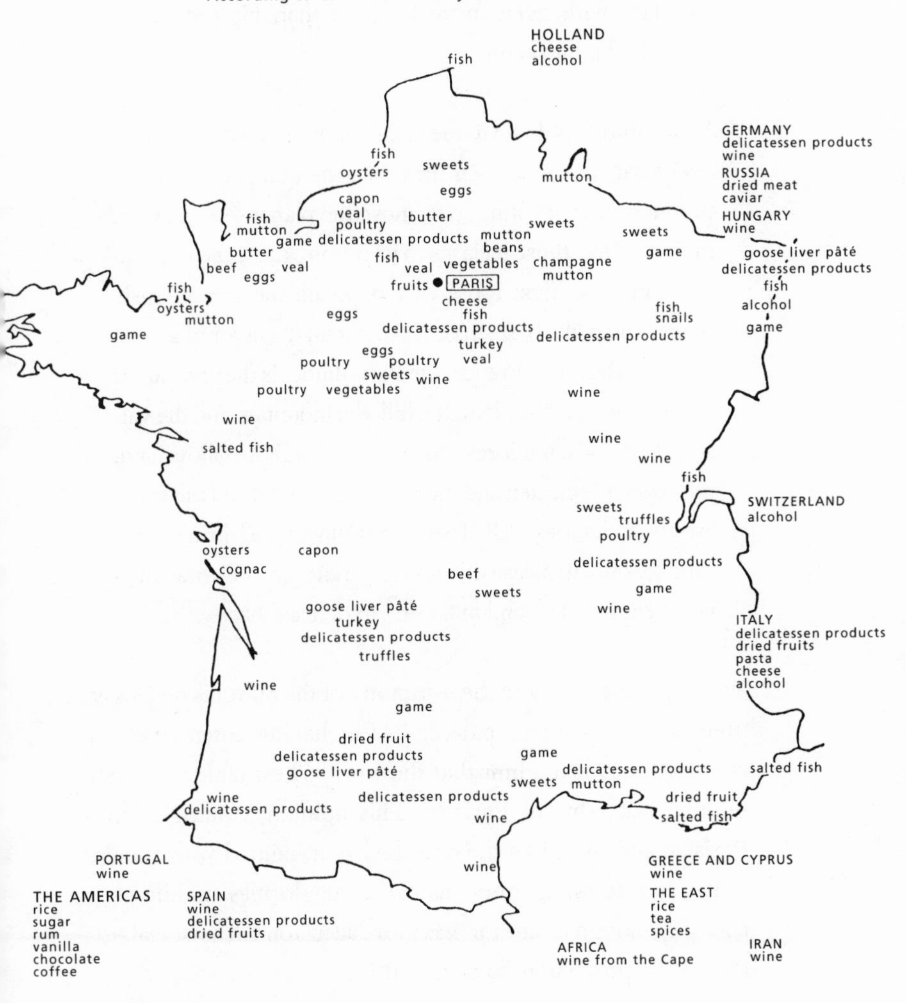

with their succulent scent."[26] Ah! That blessed time when you could receive a truffle-scented letter from Périgueux. . . .

In 1846, with even more lyricism than his predecessors, Eugène Briffault exclaims:

> When Paris sits down to the table, the entire earth stirs: from every part of the known universe, the things created, the products of every kingdom, those the planet sees growing on its surface, those it clasps to its bosom, those the sea contains and nurtures, those that populate the air: all rush, hurry, and make haste in order to obtain the favor of a look, a touch, a bite. For France, the Paris dinner is the great affair of the country. The plain, the hill, the mountain and the valley, the woods, the forest, the vineyard and the fallow land, the vegetable garden and the orchard, the land and the water are its tributaries. All desire fruitfulness and bring forth prodigy only to please this sovereign city, whose voraciousness delights them and makes them rich and happy.[27]

We could also add here the testimony of the Marquis de Cussy, prefect of Napoléon's palace: "After having eaten in every country, one must admit that the world's best table is the fine middle-class table of Paris."[28] This opinion, coming from a Parisian and thus, like the ones before it, tainted with subjectivity, is interesting only insofar as it glorifies middle-class cooking, though its author was more accustomed, by social origin and by profession, to court cuisine.

The Phenomenon of the Prince

There is no need to spell this out (and here lies the last part of the demonstration): if Paris and, by extension, all of France attained such gastronomic prestige, it was through the will of the kings and their courts. As with architecture[29] or the art of dress, the movement got under way at the time of the Italian wars, that is under the Valois, in particular François I and Henri II. The French court as it was conceived during the three centuries prior to the Revolution was the crucible for great cooking.

In Italy, where the cultural context would have permitted this development, political breakdown prevented it. In England, the other great European state to be centralized early on, the situation was entirely different. Even before Puritanism won over the ruling social strata of the country, the relatively independent aristocracy maintained itself on individual country estates—whereas *haute cuisine* is hardly possible except in the city. Stephen Mennell, who rejects the religious and moral explanation, clearly sees, on the other hand, the significance of the political and sociological factor:

> The elite was much less subject to the social forces prompting consumption for prestige purposes and displays of ever more refined tastes than the French courtiers were up until the end of the *ancien régime*. . . . In France, court society constituted a very visible caste, and its members were very preoccupied with maintaining its boundaries. The rich who were situated just outside those boundaries struggled relentlessly to be allowed in, by imitating the court's tastes and fashions.[30]

The specific nature of the French court was a matter not only of the social structure of the country's elite but also of the reigning families themselves: the alliances entered into by the monarchs, their travels abroad, and their personalities. As in the domains of literature, music, and the plastic and landscape arts, the Italian influence is fundamental, if not over cooking itself, at least over table manners. It represents a level of refinement until then unknown in France, introduced to a court at the height of its development and larger than those of the little Italian city-states where such practices had prospered in fertile soil. We must also mention the internal progress that took place throughout the Middle Ages at the royal court itself and in the most brilliant of the seignorial courts: consider the court of the lavish duke of Berry, brother of Charles V, for example, and also that of the duke of Burgundy—sometimes close, sometimes far away—in Dijon or in Flanders. They understood how the dining table is a tool of government and political influence. And then in 1495, when Charles VIII returned from Italy, victorious and dazzled, a new stage began.[31] The transformation took place throughout the sixteenth century, as much through imagination displayed at home as under the influence of the nobility's increasingly frequent trips to Italy or of Italians coming to settle in France, most prominently, the two Médicis princesses who became queens and regents of France (Catherine, wife of Henri II; Marie, wife of Henri IV).

It has often been claimed that French cooking evolved and truly took off under the direct influence of the Médicis and Italy. This is an error to which Jean-François Revel, Jean-Louis Flandrin, and many other historians have drawn attention. During the sixteenth and a good portion of the seventeenth century, French cooking at court remained very medieval in inspiration—just like Italian cooking, moreover. For example, thirty peacocks and twenty-one swans were served during a feast held in 1549 by the City of Paris for the dauphine, Catherine de Médicis. Now these fowl were served throughout the Middle Ages to honor those with power or courtly and courageous knights.[32] They later disappeared from banquet tables.

All the same, there are a few exceptions to the rule. Among them, notably, is the tentative introduction of vegetables from the other side of the Atlantic (beans, tomatoes or "apples of love," corn, Jerusalem artichokes, etc.) and especially the vogue for certain fruits and vegetables common in Italy and rare until then in France: asparagus, artichokes, cherries, strawberries, apricots, oranges, and finally melons, which achieved immense success.[33] Certain dishes at which Italian cooks were past masters were perfected: pâtés and especially sweets—fruit pastries, jams, candied fruits, nougats. In this regard, a closer study must be made of the Arab influences that came to be combined with Italian and French traditions in that crucible, the Angevin court of Naples, from which the Valois court drew part of its inspiration.[34] Apart from that, the methods of preparing meats and the recipes for sauces hardly varied.

On the other hand, proper dining customs changed profoundly under the influence of Italian refinement. Moreover, this was not something entirely new. In the thirteenth century, the manners of high Lombard society were already very elegant, as a treatise by Bonvesin de la Riva makes clear.[35] As an example, let us quote the twenty-fifth of the fifty recommended courtesies:

Here is the next one: he who shares the same plate
[with a lady
Must cut the meat for the latter and for himself.
The man must show himself to be more attentive, helpful and
[courteous
Than the shy lady ought to reasonably make him.

It is sometimes said that the presence of women at the table in France was one reason for the excellence and the refinement of its cuisine. It is certain that mixed company constituted a shield—far from being completely effective until the end of the sixteenth century—against certain guardroom behavior. This was reflected in the guests' neatness as in their conversation, and perhaps eventually in the cooking. But Renaissance France had no monopoly on this practice. In all aristocratic circles and among the upper middle classes of medieval Europe, men and women ate at the same table and were seated alternately—many miniatures of banquets offer proof of this. Segregation was only strict among the peasant classes; it remained that way in certain regions until very recently. Otherwise, we should point out that men of high society in the eighteenth century, eminent gourmets among them, liked the company of women at the table but did not make an absolute rule of it. No women participate in the famous *Déjeuner d'huitres* (*Oyster Lunch*) painted by Jean-François de Troy, and only one appears among the tipsy—and slightly slovenly—eaters in Lancret's *Déjeuner de jambon* (*Ham Lunch*).[36] Finally, there are countries, like Morocco and Japan, whose culinary refinement is indubitable and where, for a long time, the men never ate at the same table, indeed even in the same room, as the women. This is still almost general practice in Morocco and quite widespread during wedding celebrations in Japan.

The Italian treatise on good manners with the greatest influence in France at the time of the Renaissance, by Bartolomeo Sacchi (called Platine of Cremona), bore the lovely title of *De Honesta Voluptate et valetudine* (*Honest and Healthy Pleasures*) and appeared in 1474, and in French for the first time in 1505 in Lyons. It reconsiders, enlarges upon, and codifies the precepts of mannerliness already standard in the Middle Ages but not always respected, even among high society.

Among the innovations introduced at the Valois court and already winning Charles V's admiration during his December

1539 visit,[37] we find the luxury of table linens, musical accompaniment at meals—less martial than in the Middle Ages; trumpets gave up their place to lutes or coronets, more propitious for conversation—and the elegance of the guests' behavior. François I ordered the first plates in 1536.[38] Then the use of forks was imposed by Henri III, at which the *L'Isle des Hermaphrodites* visitor would laugh, wondering how to eat peas with such an instrument.[39] Murano glasses replaced metal goblets, allowing the color of wines to be appreciated. During a banquet in honor of Catherine de Médicis at the bishop's palace in Paris on June 19, 1549, the water for washing was scented, as was the cleverly folded linen, and the tables were decorated with flowers.[40] Dishes were thrown out the windows and food was thrown at other guests less often, even though the sovereigns—Charles IX, for example—sometimes allowed themselves to go overboard in this way.[41] Because despite being "His Majesty" according to the new etiquette, the monarch was no less a French gentleman, living among young lords who had not yet acquired all the good manners in fashion or who forgot them at the end of a feast with too much wine. It is hard to imagine Louis XIV trying to get the queens' ladies tipsy; as for Henri IV, however, he still took delight in doing so, by replacing their water with white wine![42] After him, such pranks would no longer be acceptable.

Louis XIV, Promoter of Haute Cuisine

As we have said—and everyone henceforth agrees on this point—aristocratic French cooking remained medieval, that is to say European, until well into the seventeenth century. At the very most, it had taken on some Italian hues. It only really developed, acquiring a true French personality, as the political and cultural prestige of France and its monarchs increased in

Europe. We must link the individualization of cooking with that of architecture, painting, sculpture, music, and landscaping. Risking a shortcut, we could link Bernini's being sent back to Italy by Louis XIV (1666) and the publication of the *Cuisinier françois* in 1651. The umbilical cord with Italy was thus cut. European cultural creations assumed the French colors in matters of gastronomy; that remains true to the present time.

We have at our disposal few documents on culinary techniques at the end of the sixteenth century and the first half of the seventeenth century, since no new recipe books appeared during this period, only earlier, reissued works. Therefore, we must believe that the old recipes were used and that cooks slowly innovated without daring to publish. In any discipline, the publication of a manual implies long labor, trials, and discussions beforehand. This is even more true of cooking, which has always engendered prescriptive and even authoritarian books: "Take. . . . Make. . . . Add. . . . It is important to. . . ." This sort of language appears in all practical works, but the conciseness of works devoted to cooking verges on caricature and thus requires the authors to be absolutely sure of themselves. That is the hypothesis we could formulate to explain the absence of culinary works between the beginning of the sixteenth and the middle of the seventeenth century.

With Henri IV, the Bourbons took their place on the throne. If the Béarnais showed himself to be a lover of simply and strongly flavored foods—garlic, for example!—taken in a friendly atmosphere, he didn't neglect to establish his prestige with great lavish banquets or to eat in public with due ceremony when etiquette required. As a child, Louis XIII benefited from an abundance and a variety of food. The journal of his doctor, Héroard,[43] reveals that he consumed every meat possible, in particular giblets, and especially poultry—Henri IV's *poule au pot* is no myth. He ate twenty-two types of fish, without counting shellfish and crustaceans; twenty-eight types of fruit, among them citrus fruits, pomegranates, and of course melons; and countless vegetables, with a predilection for asparagus, each day in spring. But, as an adult, his taciturn nature and his fragile health no more prompted him toward eating well than did his prime minister, the austere Richelieu.

Everyone knows that he was completely the opposite of his son, the gourmand all the young French learn about in history books. There were many high-living kings, indeed even reputed gluttons—like Louis VI the Fat—but Louis XIV is the only one for whom this trait is tied up with the history of his reign. It is regrettable that certain recent works get so bogged down in this one clue to the sovereign's manifold appetites. There is probably a good critical analysis to be written on the Sun King's compulsion for fine food, flesh, light, and land. . . . Versailles cuisine reflected the image of the castle and its surrounding gardens as it did the king's conception of France, radiant with butter, larded with academicism as the borders were larded by Vauban, but also as were the language, painting, sculpture, architecture, town planning, music, etc.

From childhood, Louis XIV was a glutton; he would quickly become an enlightened glutton. The energy he expended throughout his reign called for abundant food, while the heights of prestige he claimed for France required that food to be original and refined. Prosper Montagné puts it elegantly:

> If, until an advanced age, the monarch thus succeeded in meeting the requirements of a life of pomp at the same time as meeting those of all his work, without overlooking those of love, it was the most obliging of stomachs

> that always allowed him to restore his powers at the necessary moment.[44]

To support his position, he relies on Saint-Simon, who describes the king many times eating alone but most often in public, an exercise requiring a long education:

> He never lacked for appetite in his life, although he had never been hungry or really needed to eat, no matter how late he sometimes had to have dinner. But, with the first spoonfuls of soup, his appetite always returned and he ate so prodigiously and so heartily morning and night, and again so consistently, that one never got used to seeing it.[45]

And Madame Palatine, his sister-in-law, who herself had established a solid reputation for eating at Versailles, was amazed:

> I have seen the King eat, and very often eat, four bowls of different soups, a whole pheasant, a partridge, a big plate full of salad, chopped mutton in its juice with garlic, two good pieces of ham, a plate full of pastries, fruits, and preserves.[46]

Louis XIV's interest in eating well also manifested itself in the recruitment of the agronomist Jean de La Quintinie, whom he made responsible for the Versailles vegetable gardens. France's most beautiful fruits and vegetables came out of them to appear on the royal table, among them citrus fruit from the greenhouses and chasselas grapes. New varieties were selected, and the influence, abroad as well as in France, of techniques perfected there was immense.

The king's meal assumed undeniable political importance.

Actually, he generally ate alone, but he did it in public, and the ceremony surrounding that moment constituted a veritable religious ritual rendered to his being. The spectacle, ruled over by more than three hundred gentlemen, cooks, and footmen, was sought out by visitors to Versailles, where anyone could be admitted as long as he wore a sword—which could be rented. The public stayed behind the gates, and the courtiers the monarch wished to grant favors could sit on stools, a very sought-after honor from His Majesty, who sometimes spoke a kind word to them.

It was under Louis XIV's reign that a new "French" cuisine emerged. As mentioned, no new book of recipes had appeared in more than a century. In 1651, François Pierre, called La Varenne, cook for the marquis of Uxelles, published *Le Cuisinier françois* (*The French Cook*). It is the first in a series of 12 titles, or about 75, counting new editions, representing about 100,000 volumes, published up until 1691, the date of the publication of the well-known *Cuisinier royal et bourgeois* (*Royal and Middle-Class Cook*) by Français Massialot.[47] Among them are *Le Pastissier françois* (*The French Pastry Cook*), *Les Délices de la campagne* (*The Delights of the Country*), *Le Cuisinier* (*The Cook*) by Pierre de Lune, *Le Confiturier françois* (*The French Preserves Maker*) and one of the most important, very critical of certain instructions in La Varenne's work it considered archaic, *L'Art de bien traiter* (*The Art of Entertaining Well*), published in 1674 by L.S.R. Such a movement in publishing is comparable to the one we can observe in the field of architecture or grammar: the reign of Louis the Great was one of academicism and of perfecting a cultural model specifically French and exportable. It was addressed not only to the elite and its cooks but to everyone. Actually, *Le Cuisinier françois* was republished many times, beginning from 1660, in Troyes' *Bibliothèque bleue*, and in Rouen in a popular and very inexpensive edition. Through the intermediary of the peddlers, these books reached cooking professionals (innkeepers, pastry cooks, caterers, etc.) but also the entire middle class and, as Jean-Louis Flandrin and Philip and Mary Hyman have pointed out,[48] the "masters and mistresses of modest homes, in the towns and in the country, who looked to it for practical advice for their holiday meals." For all that, it is not the case that all the old habits and especially all the local customs suddenly disappeared with the spread of fashionable recipes. But that is another story . . . which remains to be written.

What did the transformations advocated by all these works consist of?[49] First of all, oriental spices, for so long the distinctive sign of wealth and nobility, and as such, used excessively in medieval cooking, were gradually reduced and replaced by French seasonings: shallots, chives, anchovies, and above all, the black truffle, which became the symbol of luxury and *haute cuisine*.

Formerly thin and dominated by tart flavors, sauces became fatty and were henceforth prepared with butter. One percent of the Taillevent recipes and not a single sauce included butter. In *L'Art de bien traiter* (1674), 55 percent of the recipes and 80 percent of the sauces contain it. Green sauce, so prized in the Middle Ages, was made of bread, parsley, ginger, verjuice, and vinegar. White sauce, very much in vogue in the eighteenth century, contained very little vinegar or spice but very much butter. It was the definitive triumph of northern France, the France of the Capetians, of dairy breeding and dairy products, over the south. Here, for example, drawn from the *Cuisinier françois*, archaic in certain respects, is the recipe for asparagus in a mild sauce:

> Choose the biggest, the ends scraped off, and wash them, then cook them in water, salt them well, and do not over-

> cook them. When cooked, set them to drain, make a sauce with very fresh butter, a little vinegar, salt, nutmeg, and one egg yolk to bind the sauce, taking care that it does not turn, and serve them garnished however you like.[50]

This is, no more no less, the recipe for asparagus with so-called hollandaise sauce, in reality very French, such as we still find in cookbooks today—or at the very least, in those a few years old, before the latest "butterphobia." Until the 1970s, butter was the distinctive sign of great French cooking, and it remains so today without always daring to speak its name.[51] In the 1950s, Fernand Point thundered his golden rule: "Butter, always butter!" And Joël Robuchon does not hesitate, even today, to prepare mashed potato purée with equal parts of butter and tubers!

Jean-Louis Flandrin comments that this growing consumption of butter could not fail to have its effects on the stoutness of members of high society. We need only compare fifteenth-century paintings and sculptures of slender virgins with art of the seventeenth century representing them as much more buxom. Cooking with butter offers an explanation. At the same time, the standards for beauty evolved; slimness was a sign of poor health and poverty, while stoutness indicated prosperity in terms of body and fortune. That would remain true until very recently for men; women gourmands have suffered more since the beginning of this century. . . .

Besides butter, pan and meat juices appear more and more often in the preparation of sauces. They are the ancestors of stocks. Massialot gives twenty-three recipes for them, each dominated by one flavor.

If the consumption of sugar continued to increase, due largely to its new availability coming from the islands, it remained concentrated in the area of confections and preserves. Parallel to that, it gradually disappeared from salty dishes. The sweet-salty combination, like the sweet and sour flavor, became vulgar, indeed even laughable. There are not many vestiges of ancient medieval cooking left today: at the most, a few white meat or game dishes with prunes or cranberry preserves, duck in orange sauce, sweet mutton tarts from Pézanas, and the bit of sugar added when cooking peas.

There is probably much to be said about this segregation of flavors. Seventeenth-century works defend the natural taste of products, the taste that overcooking, spices, acids, and sugar (but not butter!) would supposedly hide.

> Such meat asks for a vinaigrette, a vinaigrette sauce with pepper; that depends only on taste, but to tell you the truth, the best and the healthiest way of eating roast meat is devouring it right from the spit in its natural juices and not completely cooked, without applying so many inconvenient precautions, which in their strange fashion destroy the true taste of things.[52]

Whereby we see that the only thing new about the late twentieth century's "new" cuisine is the adjective!

The proliferation of simmered dishes and *coulies* or sauces bound with a roux or butter rendered the traditional organization of kitchens inadequate. Since the Middle Ages, the essential part of food preparation had taken place before the hearth, where you could roast, or boil in a cooking pot suspended from a trammel. You could also cook under the ashes. To keep a sauce warm or stew a dish, all you had at your disposal were pots set above the andirons into which were placed a handful of live coals, tripods set over the embers, and sometimes niches cut into the walls of the chimney. Castles and important residences were furnished with ovens that served, in particular, for cooking pâtés. Before the fire, you bent over or squatted down, or sometimes stood to do the roasting when there were quite a number of spits on the grill.

The great eighteenth-century revolution in the organization of French kitchens was the *potager*, ancestor to the stove or kitchen range. It was not, properly speaking, a novelty, because it already existed in Italy a century before, as we can witness in the description of the ideal culinary setup advocated by Bartolomeo Scappi, secret cook for Pope Pius V in 1570.[53] This type of arrangement came into general use over the course of the century.[54] The *potager* was built out of bricks sometimes covered with earthenware tiles, and contained one or many stoves that were filled with hot coals. The ashes fell through a grill and were collected in an ash pan. There you prepared and set the *potages*, that is, broths filled with meats, vegetables, and various other things,[55] sauces, ragoûts, braised meats, and all dishes that needed careful attention. A portable copper stove, also supplied with coals, may have supplemented the *potager*. This new cooking box was placed as close as possible to a window, in order to avoid the noxious effects of carbon monoxide put off by the hot coals.

Henceforth, cooking was done standing up, close to the source of heat, a position more favorable for producing complicated hot dishes. This advantage was lost when dishes were presented on pedestals and feathers were restored to the fowl as in the Middle Ages, a long and painstaking operation. Then, food was eaten lukewarm, indeed even cold. That was one of the major inconveniences of what would gradually be called "French service," in which many dishes were brought to the table for the guests to consume in any order they wished, either serving themselves or asking waiters to give them this or that piece. It is this type of service that Master Jacques discusses with his master Harpagon when it comes to preparing a fine meal that the latter would prefer to be more rustic and less extravagant:

> Harpagon: First we must have some of those things that one hardly eats and that first satisfy one's appetite: a few good beans, well-buttered, with some potted pâté well filled with chestnuts. There, let's have plenty.
>
> . . . .
>
> Master Jacques: All right, we will need four large soups and five plates. Soups. . . . Entrées. . . . Roast. . . . Desserts. . . .[56]

The clearest sign of how *haute cuisine* influenced middle-class and even peasant cooking was this "*potager* revolution." The new system was adopted by all families, in towns as well as in the country.[57] Through the estate inventories done between 1620 and 1790, we can see it spread to Paris.[58] Potagers dating from this period still exist in many Burgundian houses, the most modest being cut into the wall located at the back of the hearth, in which case they are called *cendriers*, or ash pans.[59] Thus, even if the recipes in the *Cuisinier françois*, distributed by the *Bibliothèque bleue*, were not all used, some of them could be without difficulty, even in the thatched cottages.[60] One of the most beautiful eighteenth-century kitchens, preserved in its original state, belonged to the marchioness of Cabris and can still be seen today in Grasse, at the Fragonard Museum. The huge hood shelters both a raised hearth and a *potager* with several stoves.

Along with the evolution of tastes and kitchens, table manners continued to be refined, at least at the court and in its sphere of influence. Even if the king and nobility still ate in their antechambers, this act had become too important not to warrant a room of its own: the dining room, provided with a fixed table—no longer trestle tables set up for each meal—assorted chairs, a cupboard, and various improvements meant to serve and charm guests: a fountain for refreshing drinks, a sideboard, a reach-through cut into a wall or sometimes into the floor so that, in the latter case, for example, the table could arrive from the kitchen replete with dishes. Certain lords, who formerly took their meals in the kitchen with their servants or in their chambers, now fitted out a special room[61] for what became a little ceremony, a distant echo of the production and the king's royal protocol at Versailles. But not until the nineteenth century did the dining room come into general use. In many middle-class homes, it then became the show room where guests were received if there was no space for a sitting room. Today, it has often disappeared to be replaced by a living room–sitting room with a small eating corner.

In the same way, the perfecting of table arts that began with the Renaissance continued. At the court and in high society, each guest was provided with as many plates, place settings, glasses, and napkins as he desired. The teams for cooking and serving numbered more, on great occasions, than the guests. Here again is a practice preserved in our own time in great restaurants; it is, of course, what explains in part the price of a meal in such establishments. Formerly imported, from Italy in particular, all the dishes were henceforth made in France, often with royal privilege, before the king himself created manufacturers. This was the case with the delicate porcelain from Rouen, manufactured by Edme Poterat beginning in 1673; and that same year, M. Perrot's porcelain in Orleans; and that of Saint-Cloud in 1677. Later came Vincennes in 1725, then Chantilly before Sèvres, the first French manufacturer of hard porcelain, founded in 1745. In addition to the French ware, hard porcelains from China penetrated France as early as the late fifteenth century. The expansion of earthenware and porcelain production was motivated by the melting down of precious dishes in an effort to bail the state out of financial difficulties in 1689, 1699, 1709, and 1759.[62] Silverware remained very prized nonetheless, either by foreign courts or for gifts given by the king, and naturally one turned to silversmiths for forks and spoons. Glassworks proliferated, but lead crystal, invented in England in 1615, would not be made in the royal factories of Saint-Louis, Sèvres, Baccarat, and Cruesot until the second half of the eighteenth century.

The final sign of the cultural status that the art of eating well had earned in France under Louis XIV's reign: conversation. It was not improper to speak of fine food or of cooks. The lines written by Madame de Maintenon in 1696 with regard to peas are well known: "The impatience for eating them, the pleasure of having eaten them, and the joy of eating them again, are the three points that I have been meaning to treat for three days."[63] It is true that, besides the king's, the court contained a few hearty appetites. The duchess of Berry would even die of indigestion.[64]

From the Royal Table to the Republican Banquet

We can well imagine that the king's public meals and the great extravaganzas served at celebrations were hardly propitious for the exchange of confidences and the expression of feelings. Certainly gastronomy was a delight for the senses, but above all, it was a service for the prince and the image that he sought to project of himself. As Brillat-Savarin would later say, "meals became a means of government."[65] And of diplomacy, we could add. Only the small late suppers and the delicate meals taken in the garden (light refreshments, cold buffets) permitted more intimacy.

The Regent and then King Louis XV maintained the complicated ceremony of Louis XIV's reign. However, they managed more moments of intimacy; that is, they supped, when they could, with a few of those close to them, counting among them, if possible, some gracious and witty ladies.[66] The dishes ordered and served hot thus reflected the prince's tastes more than etiquette. The latter did not disdain, on occasion, cooking for himself—or pretending to, as Marie Antoinette played at farming—thus multiplying his pleasure and that of his guests. Sparkling champagne became the essential drink to accompany these meals. Its bubbles were associated in the imagination with lightness, joy, and luxury. It had long been forbidden to the Sun King by his doctor, Fagon, who considered it too acid and recommended instead the wine from Vosne (cut with water, according to the custom of the time), thus looking after his own interests, since he was a native of Nuits![67]

That exquisite version of *haute cuisine*, the little supper, was adopted enthusiastically by all polite society. Many engravings and paintings offer proof of that. By this time, gastronomy had entered into normal French custom, so it was practiced by all, including the philosophers who, in a word, protested the political structure that gave birth to it. This paradox would culminate during the French Revolution.

From then on, the pattern was established. The gastronomic torch would be transmitted systematically up to the present day and through all the various governments—monarchies, empires, republics—by the highest state dignitaries. Louis XVI inherited the Bourbons' gluttony, to the point of being sick with indigestion on the day of his wedding (the wedding night spoiled!). He contributed to the popularity of the potato, a basic food for the common people, destined to banish the specter of famine. To do this, he organized with Parmentier a gastronomic ceremony to ennoble the tuber scorned by the French: a meal with a menu featuring many potato dishes. For this occasion, the king wore a bouquet of potato flowers as a boutonniere and spoke these vibrant words of praise for Parmentier: "Men such as you are not recompensed with silver. There is a kind of currency more worthy of them. Give me your hand and kiss the queen."[68] With the stratagem of the Sablons, general support would be won for good.

But the king also used all his prestige to promote a luxury product: Strasbourg foie gras.[69] Probably already prepared by the Jewish community in Alsace, pâté de foie gras was perfected, the tradition maintains, by Jean-Pierre Clause, cook for the Alsace commander-in-chief, the marshal of Contades. The latter offered it to the king, who was delighted with it and offered it in turn almost throughout Europe. Clause settled into his furnished rooms in 1784 and his fortune was made, like that of the Strasbourg pâtés, which became a sort of national symbol. Dining in the company of the Tsarevich, Guillaume I, and Bismarck on June 7, 1867 at the Café Anglais, Tsar Alexander II declared himself deeply disappointed not to find foie gras on the menu. Claudius Burdel—the grandfather of Claude Terrail, present owner of the Tour d'Argent—explained that this was not the season for it and, to save his honor, the following winter sent his guests a "Three Kings foie gras," obviously prepared according to the Strasbourg recipe: an excellent example of the know-how and ingenuity of French cooks and of the French in general, with regard to their gastronomy.

This close relationship between the taste of the kings and their courts and the promotion of gastronomic products as well as their recipes is very old. We have already noted it for wines, and we can do the same for certain cheeses. There is no end, for example, to the list of connections between Brie and the princes.[70] As early as 1217, the countess of Champagne, Blanche de Navarre, offered two hundred such cheeses to Philippe Auguste. In 1407, Charles d'Orléans had about twenty dozen sent as presents; then came Henri IV, the Grand Condé, who offered them at the end of the battle of Rocroi; Mari Leczinska used Brie, it is said, to make her famous "*bouchées à la reine*"; Louis XVI. . . . The final—and international—consecration occurred over the course of the Congress of Vienna.[71] Talleyrand proposed organizing a European cheese competition, and the Brie that he submitted was hailed as the king of cheeses, before fifty-two contestants, among them Lord Castlereagh's Chester, Metternich's Bohemian cheese, and the Nesselrode's cheese from Livonia.

Like Brie, Roquefort has benefited from much royal backing since the Middle Ages. In 1457, Charles VII ratified, through a charter, an ancient tradition: the right of the inhabitants of the village of Roquefort to levy a tax on the cheeses that all the area's dairy farmers "in the summertime are used to bringing to said cellars where the said cheeses are made and become good and flavorful." The charter was confirmed by François I in 1518, and then by several more sovereigns up to Louis XIV in 1645.

The legend of Camembert, the national emblem,[72] is prosaic and imperial at the same time, and even if it is not true, it deserves to be. . . .[73] In the eighteenth century, this cheese was still very local, only available at the Vimoutiers market. Marie Harel was born in Brie in 1761. Tradition holds that she applied to the cheese of Camembert, the Norman village where she settled, the methods used in Brie. She succeeded marvelously, kept shop in Argentan, and then passed her expertise on to her daughter. That is when the decisive event took place, the catalyst for its reputation! Thomas Paynel, her son-in-law, went off to Surdon and, on the day of the inauguration of the Paris-Granville railroad line, offered the cheese to Napoléon III, who declared himself enchanted by it, demanded that his table at Tuileries always be provided with it, and went so far as to receive Paynel at the palace. . . .[74]

Napoléon I's attitude clearly illustrates the henceforth indissoluble bond between the state and gastronomy in France. His own tastes, inherited from a quite rustic upbringing and a youth passed in barracks or on the battlefields, led him more toward fatty meats, soups of bread and beans, and macaroni, washed down with Chambertin much diluted with ice water, than toward the *haute cuisine* inherited from the *ancien régime*.[75] Nevertheless, conscious of the importance of outward signs of power and prestige, he explicitly entrusted to Cambacérès and especially Talleyrand—who both took obvious pleasure in it—the responsibility of entertaining state guests. It was in preparing the Empire's extravaganzas that Antonin Carême codified the recipes for great French cooking.

Carême is one of the most well-known figures in the history of gastronomy. After Massialot, other cooks employed in court circles had published works refining, detailing, and contradicting, sometimes with scant ceremony, their predecessors: for example, *Les Dons de Comus* (*The Gifts of Comus*) by François Marin in 1739, *Le Cuisinier moderne* (*The Modern Cook*) by Vincent La Chapelle in 1742, *La Cuisinière bourgeoise* (*The Middle-Class Cook*), and *Les Soupers de la cour* (*The Court Suppers*) by Menon in 1746 and 1755. Carême goes even further in the complexity of his recipes, the luxury of his ingredients, and the attention he gives to the marriage of flavors. Above all, he especially represents the culmination of expertise in matters of presentation for dishes and buffets. This constant raising of the stakes that accompanied the apotheosis of great French service—the only kind Carême considered worthy of the high and mighty—actually signaled its death. First, the cost was prohibitive, and second, the food was cold, or lukewarm at best. So-called Russian service—introduced in 1810 by Prince Kourakine, the Russian ambassador—with hot dishes presented successively, gradually gained favor and became widely accepted under the Second Empire. French service survives in the buffets of today's great caterers, whose art can be directly linked to Carême's. Rather than meals as such, these buffets are, moreover, the heirs to the *ambigus*, cold buffets served late in the evening.

As an itinerant cook, Carême directed the kitchens of Alexander I, the prince of Galles, the princess Bagration, and the baron of Rothschild. While he was in Paris, he provided all the special banquets for Napoléon, Talleyrand, and Louis XVIII, who authorized him to call himself Carême of Paris. Worthy of the Bourbon name, Louis XVIII greatly appreciated fine food, although it meant suffering from gout. It was said that he could recognize the origin of a wild rabbit without fail from the first mouthful, an ability recalling the seventeenth-century talents of Dom Pérignon: the storeroom keeper for the abbey of Hautvillers could supposedly name the source of grape clusters from tasting them, and assembled the champagne vintages with infallible knowledge, or more accurately, with exceptional sensitivity.

It was Carême who arranged meals for the French delegation to the Congress of Vienna, led by Talleyrand. "Sire," the prince responded to Louis XVIII, who kept giving him more advice, "I need casseroles more than written instructions."

Carême threatened to leave Talleyrand for another house in Vienna, but the latter knew how to convince him to continue "serving France." And François Bonneau amusingly concludes, "Carême retained his kitchens; France retained its borders."[76]

Carême was a fanatic about writing. Wherever he went, each evening he noted his culinary experiences and commented on them. Though self-taught, he spent long hours in the royal library copying out the architectural designs he then used as inspiration for creating the centerpieces and pedestals of which he was master. His published work is enormous for a cook who was so active as well: *Le Pâtissier pittoresque* (*The Colorful Pastry Cook*) (1815), *Le Maître d'Hôtel français* (*The French Maître d'Hôtel*) (1822), *Le Cuisinier parisien* (*The Parisian Cook*) (1828), *L'Art de la Cuisine française au XIX*e *siècle* (*The Art of French Cooking in the Nineteenth Century*) (three volumes in 1833, two posthumous volumes in 1843–44). His influence on cooking would only be surpassed three quarters of a century later, by Escoffier.[77]

Carême was also the first true cooking star. Before him, there was Taillevent; then Vatel, the *maitre d'* for Fouquet (that is, more a steward than a cook) and then for the prince of Condé, whose suicide at Chantilly was immortalized by Madame de Sévigne's account: "He fell over dead. The tide nevertheless arrived from all sides. . . . Gourville tried to make up for Vatel's loss; she succeeded: they dined very well."[78] Also there was André Noël, Perigordian cook for Frederick the Great, king of Prussia.[79] Carême surpassed them all in notoriety and perhaps also in self-importance. This fault is apparent with all cooks, at least beginning with La Varenne, but Carême took delight in cultivating it. In his manner of writing, of constantly praising himself and judging his colleagues or predecessors, he prefigures some of the "great divas" of the twentieth century. In addition, he had absolutely no sense of humor. In reading him, we are reminded of what the novelist, Fanny Deschamps, later wrote about her dear nephew, the late Alain Chapel:

> The cook is a mass of emotional flesh wrapped in an extraordinary delicate skin of pride. A true Bresse capon skin: lay a finger on it lacking a ounce of respect and you'll leave a bruise.[80]

After the fall of Napoléon III, we know the extent to which the successive presidents of the Republic were committed to maintaining the tradition by how lavishly they entertained their foreign guests, but also by the way they marked their promotions to the head of state with gastronomic ceremonies. The most spectacular of these was the banquet for the mayors of France given at the Tuileries on September 22, 1900 during the International Exposition and attended by 23,000 French mayors. Potel and Chabot worked wonders and served a dozen dishes. The collection of works entitled *The Thirty Days That Made France* would devote a thirty-first volume to this September 22, because there, in the Gallic and Germanic tradition, the apotheosis of national unity was celebrated at the table. A recent attempt to repeat it brought together 15,000 individuals on the lawns of Rueilly on October 28, 1987, gathered around then Prime Minister Jacques Chirac. Nine thousand of these were mayors from all the parties, about a quarter of the highest local French officials. That is not so bad for a period less attached than its precursors to patriotic gatherings, but not entirely disdaining them if there is some chance that the table will be well spread.

Another recent event, among so many others, testifies to the preservation of the French principles of governing at the table: the presentation of the Legion of Honor ribbon to Paul Bocuse by President Valéry Giscard d'Estaing in 1975. The ceremony took place over the course of a meal prepared by the most prominent chefs at the time (Guérard, Verger, Troisgros, and a few others). For the occasion, Bocuse created a virtuosic new dish, henceforth a permanent item on his menu: *la soupe de truffe VGE.*

One might think that with the left coming into power in 1981, politics and casseroles would become confused, or at the very least, that *haute cuisine*, belonging to the "people of the castle," as Prime Minister Pierre Mauroy said, would be sacrificed on the alter of populism. The temptation was strong, and for a year or two, picnics were held here and there in the ministries. And then nature rushed back in and eating well reclaimed its rights. Jack Lang, Minister of Culture, and his colleague in Agriculture, Henri Nallet, entrusted to the journalist Jean Ferniot the responsibility of putting together a report on the future of gastronomy. Many great cooks received either the Legion of Honor, the *Mérite*, or the Arts and Letters award, and President Mitterand inaugurated a Place Jean-Troisgros in Roanne. Although lighter than a century before, the Elysée cuisine was no less in keeping with court cuisine with regard to the rarity of the dishes served and the elaborate preparations, not to mention the wines chosen from among the wine cellar's 15,000 great bottles. Joël Normand, head of the kitchens, hides nothing:[81] "The president is faithful to a certain culinary tradition. . . . The president likes to begin with shellfish or fish, and after that, lamb, a poultry dish, milk-fed veal, a dish created like a *vol-au-vent à la financière*." The guests of France certainly did not understand that it could be otherwise and would have been offended at being served some ordinary snack. "The Elysée table," writes Nicolas de Rabaudy, "is France's showcase. It offers a certain image of the national destiny, the art of living, of receiving and entertaining its guests."[82]

Finally, let us recall an anecdote going back to the 1988 presidential campaign. For a time, the Socialist Party had kept out of things a bit, so as not to lose the centrist voters. The moment came, that is, April 13, 1988, for the presidential candidate to reassure his old guard. What better place to pull off such a family gathering than at the table? Here is the account given by *Le Monde*:

> The place for these feasts? A temple—unrecognized—of gastronomy, Le Pouilly-Reuilly, at Pré-Saint-Gervais (Seine-Saint-Denis), for which the mayor, the Socialist Marcel Debarge, a regular client, is an effective propagandist. There are eighteen at the table. . . . M. Thibault, host, explains in detail the president's menu to the four journalists who have rushed to the scene: eggs *enmeurette*, whole veal kidneys with shallots, with sautéed apples and fresh morels, strawberries, all served with a Saint-Emilion *grand cru*—a 1982 Château-Soutard—and a 1981 Roederer champagne. Leaving, the president pronounced a few historic words: "This is a good restaurant."[83]

"Francogastria"

A few years ago, Francophonia became a battle horse for French cultural institutions and politics. It is talked about much more now than in the period when French was the language of all the European elite. We do not talk about "Francogastria"—a terribly ugly word that almost looks like a disease!—that is, the French way of eating well, and so much the better, because the latter still goes almost without saying in much of the country, as soon as one tries to find fine food.

Theodore Zeldin is wrong when he traces the international reputation of French cuisine back only to the beginning of the nineteenth century.[84] In fact, it dates back to the seventeenth century. *Le Cuisinier françois* was translated into English as early as 1653, two years after it was published in France, and then into German and Italian (six editions by 1815). The same is true of *Cuisinier royal et bourgeois* and many other works. In his preface, Massialot writes without modesty and without any doubt, because the fact is recognized abroad, at least in court circles: "We can pride ourselves in France on having the edge over other nations in cooking. . . . My book can be very good evidence of what I propose."[85] In 1687, a German named Tomasius complained, "Today, at home, everything must be French. Clothes, words, furniture. . . . There is not even anything bad that is French that is not the exclusive fashion."[86]

All the European sovereigns recruited French cooks by offering them small fortunes. We could cite, for example, Vincent La Chapelle, an itinerant cook who officiated in England, Holland, Germany, Portugal, on ships, and in the East Indies, as well as at Louis XV's court. His *Cuisinier moderne*, in five volumes, was first published in English in London in 1733, and then in French in Paris in 1742. He was the inventor of "*sauce espagnole*," for a long time the base for a multitude of other sauces. The most famous of expatriate cooks is undoubtedly André Noël, who directed the kitchen for Frederick II, the king of Prussia.[87] Born in Périgueux in 1726, he entered into the service of the Berlin sovereign in 1755, as provisions officer under the orders of the Lyonnais cook, Joyard. In 1764, Casanova described him as "a very cheerful man . . . who was the only and dearly beloved cook of His Prussian Majesty." Not all the dishes he prepared were French, but a certain number of them were, such as that "*bombe de Sardanapale*," a stuffed cabbage, still prepared today in Périgord and elsewhere in France, served in 1772 and earning its creator an ode from the king in 137 lines: "Today, Sir Noël, you outdid yourself! Oh! That *bombe de Sardanapale* was a marvel of taste, was a dish of the gods!"

In about the same period, Clouet, in the service of the duke of Newcastle, was a celebrity across the Channel, and then entered the service of Marshal Richelieu once he returned to the country.[88] Throughout the eighteenth and nineteenth centuries, French cooks continued to expatriate voluntarily, but, despite their comfortable remunerations, they were not as stable as Noël. Carême flitted from the tsar's kitchens to those of the prince of Galles in Brighton. In the 1860s, the kitchens of the Prussian king were directed alternately by Urbain Dubois and Emile Bernard, whose published work, in French as well as in translation, is enormous and all the more influential since the recipes in it are explained in very precise detail. Escoffier invited a great number of young cooks to expatriate, but his sphere of influence is more that of the luxury hotels than of official kitchens.

There is a good chance that the meal offered at Windsor on March 13, 1879 to the Tsarina Marie by Queen Victoria was prepared under the direction of a French chef.[89] Everything about it was French, including the language in which the menu was written, except the beef and game, which, at the end of the preceding century, Arthur Young himself had declared England's way of preparing to be one of its rare culinary superiorities over France:[90]

> SOUPS, à la reine, à la tortue, à la royale; FISH, Turbot with Lobster Sauce, Fried Filets of Sole; ENTREES, Chicken Croquettes *à la D'Artois*, Mutton Cutlets *à la Soubise*, Stuffed Wings *à la bohémienne*; RELEVES, Chicken with Mixed Vegetables, Roast Beef, Haunch of Venison; ROASTS, Duckling, Chicken; DESSERTS, Artichokes *à la Lyonnaise*, Chocolate Glazed Biscuits, Aspic garnished with Fruit; RELEVE, Brioche Crusts with Apricots.

French cooks employed by the world's rich and powerful are less numerous today, and even rather rare. There is an important reason for that: reigning families with almost unlimited income have become rare, with the exception of those in the Middle East where, furthermore, a few French do officiate, and certain banana republics where the presidential budget is readily confused with that of the state. Olav V, the king of Norway, was familiar with French cooks in the royal palace of Oslo in his parents' time. Today, they are Norwegian, but the official banquets maintain a style inspired by French customs. S. G. Sender, a pastry cook originally from Belgium but living in France, where he creates masterpieces in the style of Carême and advises Gaston Lenôtre, is the latest in a line of nomadic pastry cooks having officiated in Russia, Prussia, and Thailand since 1824. He himself directed the special events at Buckingham Palace at the time of George VI.[91] Today, many official palace cooks travel, take training courses, and can therefore learn French methods through their education or the course of their careers. This is nothing new. That is why etiquette forbade—and no doubt still does—the emperor of Japan to be served by foreigners; but, after Meiji, official banquets given at the palace were often in the French style and prepared by chefs trained in the French style.

Akisawa Tokuzo, the cook for emperor Taisho, learned his art in France. Here is the menu he prepared on the occasion of the coronation, November 17, 1916 (that is, four years after the reign began) for two thousand people. There is only a single nod to the Empire's traditional cuisine: the steam! Turtle consommé, crayfish soup (collected at Hokkaido and Nikko by the army), trout steamed with sake, steamed chicken, grilled beef filet, cold partridge, orange and wine sorbet, roast turkey, salad, cooked celery, ice cream, dessert, served with amontillado, Château d'Yquem 1900, Château-Margaux 1877, Clos-Vougeot 1899, Pommery champagne, coffee, and cognac.[92] Still today in Japan, toasts are drunk with champagne at the end of official banquets given by the emperor.

What has been true of cooks and cooking techniques for more than three centuries is equally true of the basic products that allow French *haute cuisine* meals to be made. Besides the wines, which are easily preserved and transported, for a long time now France has exported pâtés, foie gras in particular; salt meat or fish; jams and various sweets; cheeses; high-quality fruits and vegetables (especially since the coming of railroads); fine preserves, etc. Today, as we know, these exports have taken on major economic importance.

Likewise, the productions of French table arts have crossed borders since the reign of Louis XIV. Until that time, dining room decor was Italianate or still medieval (tapestries hung over stone walls); the most beautiful glassware was from Venice, England, or Bohemia; the most beautiful silverware was often German, especially in the East; and porcelain was Chinese. Gradually, French objects, or imitations of them, appeared throughout: in Sans-Souci, Caserte, Queiluz, Saint Petersburg, etc. After Lisbon was destroyed in 1755, Joseph I of Portugal ordered a 1,274–piece silver service from the Parisian silversmith, F.-Th. Germain.[93] Today in Copenhagen's Amalienborg palace, we can see the reproduction of the table where, on January 29, 1770, King Christian VII served dinner at the castle of Christianborg in Copenhagen.[94] Everything there is French: the paintings are by Boucher and Le Tocqué, the wood paneling and decorations by Le Clerc, the silver by Louis XV's silversmith, Thomas Germain, who lived in the Galeries du Louvre. Most of the pieces have been preserved, with the exception of the centerpieces weighing as much as 61 kilograms.

Thus blessed by the Church and granted prestige by the highest authorities of the state, *haute cuisine* made an ever larger place for itself in the cultural universe of the French. Born in high circles, the phenomenon won over all levels of society in a way that remains to be understood. Even if they did not have daily access to it, people knew what it involved, imagined it, and sometimes sampled it at home, thanks to cookbooks and caterers, or at a restaurant, that profoundly French institution that has distinguished itself from all other establishments on the planet.

1. The Evrault tower harbors the kitchens of the Fontevrault abbey (twelfth century). GIRAUDON

2. The interior of the kitchens in the Dijon ducal palace, built in 1433 for Philippe the Good. Like those in Fontevrault, these kitchens were especially designed for roasting and for boiling, and hardly or not at all for simmering. LAUROS-GIRAUDON

3. The table of a banquet presided over by the duke of Berry (*Les Très Riches Heures du duc de Berry*, fifteenth century). Chantilly, Condé Museum. GIRAUDON

4. A pessimistic vision of gourmandism, carved on the portal of the Sainte-Foy de Conques abbey (eleventh century). The demons are forcing the gourmand to vomit all he has ingested over the course of his life. Such threats hurled by the preachers had little effect in France. MICHEL HAYAUX DU TILLY

5. In Hieronymus Bosch's image, the sin of gourmandism is presented from a more pleasant perspective. Detail from the *Table of Capital Sins* (fifteenth century). Prado . X.D.R.

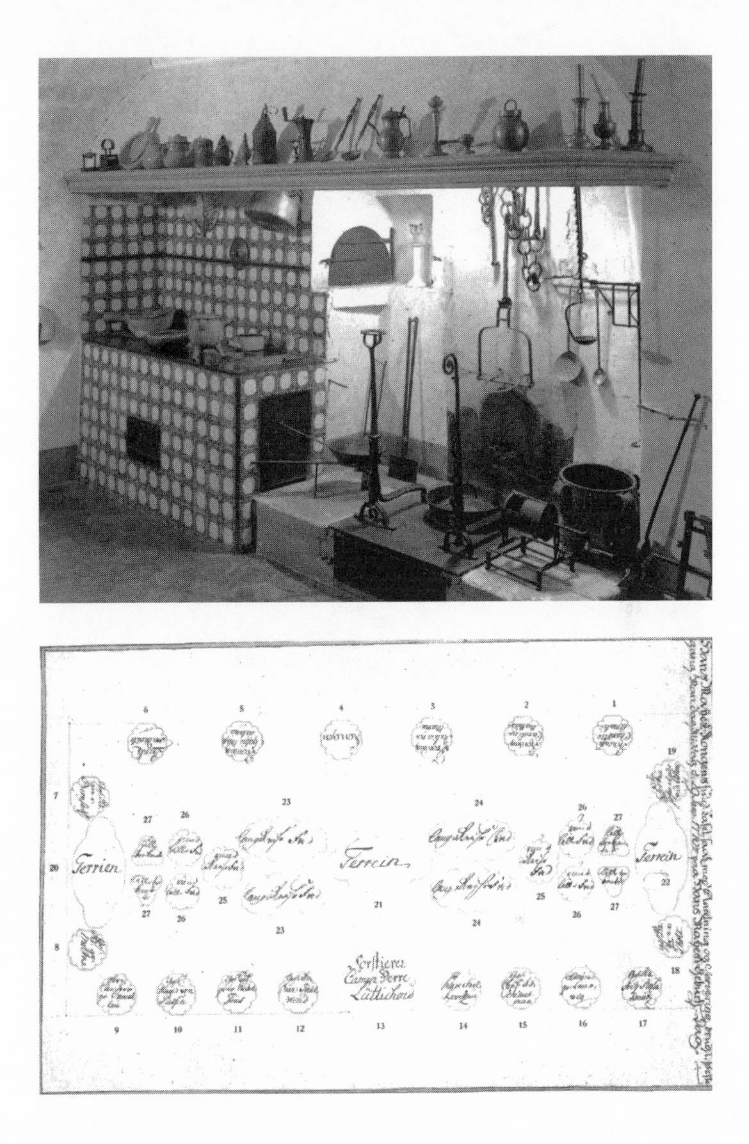

6. The kitchens of the Cabris hotel (1774), now at the Fragonard Museum in Grasse. Beside the earthen hearth, a medieval tradition, a potager allows simmered dishes and sauces to be made. LAUROS-GIRAUDON

7. The table plan for the dinner prepared on January 29, 1770, on the occasion of the twenty-first birthday of Christian VII, king of Denmark. The silverware, essentially Parisian, allowed the dishes to be splendidly presented, according to the principles of great "French" service. DENMARK NATIONAL ARCHIVES

8. Supper menu served to Louis XV and Mme. de Pompadour at the Choisy castle on November 4, 1757. HARLINGUE-VIOLLET

9, Complex presentations for poultry (*chaud-froid*, with truffles, etc.) recommended by Urbain Debois at the end of the nineteenth century. The last gasps of the decorative cuisine inherited from the *ancien régime*. SPECIAL COLLECTION

10. Luncheon given by Louis-Phillippe for Queen Victoria in the Eu forest on September 6, 1843; the meal was served in front of onlookers gathering to enjoy the show. Painting by K. Girardet, Versailles Museum. LAUROS-GIRAUDON

11. The banquet served to the mayors of France by President Loubet on September 22, 1900, marking the height of political and cultural unity in France. HARLINGUE-VIOLLET

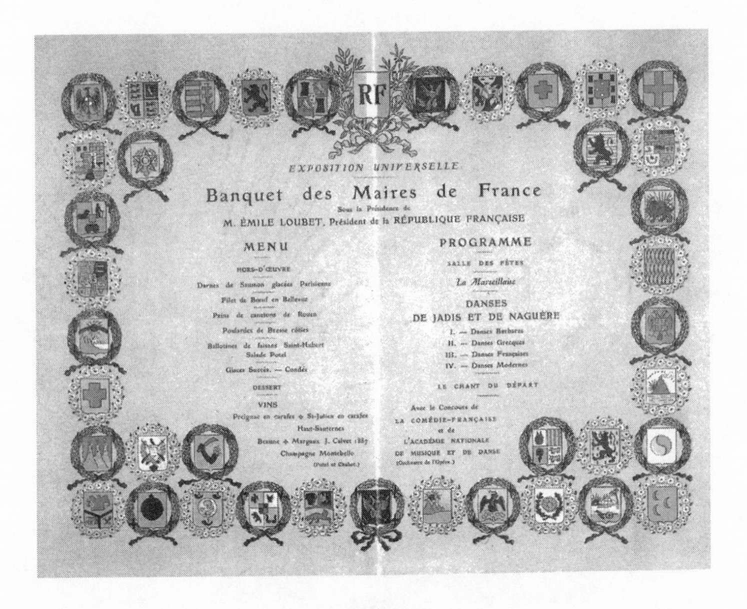

RF

EXPOSITION UNIVERSELLE

Banquet des Maires de France

Sous la Présidence de

M. ÉMILE LOUBET, Président de la RÉPUBLIQUE FRANÇAISE

MENU

HORS-D'ŒUVRE

Darnes de Saumon glacées Parisienne

Filet de Bœuf en Bellevue

Pains de canetons de Rouen

Poulardes de Bresse rôties

Ballotines de faisans Saint-Hubert
Salade Potel

Glaces Succès. — Condés

DESSERT

VINS

Preignac en carafes ✤ St-Julien en carafes

Haut-Sauternes

Beaune ✤ Margaux J. Calvet 1887

Champagne Montebello

(Potel et Chabot.)

PROGRAMME

SALLE DES FÊTES

La Marseillaise

DANSES
DE JADIS ET DE NAGUÈRE

I. — Danses Barbares

II. — Danses Grecques

III. — Danses Françaises

IV. — Danses Modernes

LE CHANT DU DÉPART

Avec le Concours de

LA COMÉDIE-FRANÇAISE

et de

L'ACADÉMIE NATIONALE

DE MUSIQUE ET DE DANSE

(Orchestre de l'Opéra.)

12. The menu for the French mayors' banquet. Wines and dishes came from all over France. KHARBINE/TAPABOR

13. Gastronomic map of France, designed and engraved by Torcaty, from *Dîners de Manantville* by Ch. L. Cadet de Gassicourt (1809). BHVP

Bruges
Lille
Bruxelles
Namur
Coblentz
Mayence
LORRAINE
Abbeville
Neufchatel
Rouen
Pontoise
Montmorency
BRIE
Epernay
Rheims
Verdun
Metz
Phalsbourg
Strasbourg
Nancy
St. Germain en laye
PARIS
Melun
Meaux
Chalons
Versailles
Chartres
Fontainebleau
Troyes
Bar
Pithiviers
Orléans
Langres
Coulanges
Chablis
BOURGOGNE
Dijon
Besançon
Bourges
Nevers
Beaune
Gruyere
Genève
Macon
Clermont
Limoges
Lyon
PUY DE DÔME
Grenoble
St. Flour
Roquefort
l'Hermitage
Grasse
Nismes
Arles
Montpellier
Aix
Nice
Marseille
Narbonne
Perpignan

14. Luncheon given at l'Elysée by M. and Mme. Mitterand for the king and queen of Spain on December 7, 1988. The French willingly accept the idea of expenses incurred for prestigious meals. SIMON

15. The team that presides over the organization of official meals at l'Elysée Palace. SIMON

16. Official reception given by the emperor Hirohito in honor of the Brazilian president Geisel. The table is organized in the French style; toasts are made with champagne. X.D.R.

17. Japanese service: many dishes in small quantities; importance given to the arrangement of colors; dishes frequently covered. J.-R. PITTE

18. Zucchini mousse served at L'Oustau de Baumanière. The influence of Japanese presentation is very clear here. J.-R. PITTE

19. French cuisine interpreted by a Japanese chef. X.D.R.

20. Illuminated advertisement in the Tokyo metro for the gastronomic products of the Troisgros brothers. J.-R. PITTE

21. One of the first chefs to descend into the media arena: Raymond Oliver, on the television show, *Art et magie de la cuisine*. SFP–DANIEL FALLOT

22. A Parisian event: the funeral of Roger Cazes, owner of the Lipp brasserie, January 30, 1987. GAILLARDE/GAMMA

23. Grand traditional cuisine served at Maxim's, one of the most famous restaurants on the planet. BEINAMON/EDELHAJT-GAMMA

24. Dinner theater: Maxim's restaurant in Nice, situated in an old theater. The kitchen is set up on the stage, and the curtain is raised at the end of the meal. J.-R. PITTE

25. Michel Guérard in front of the street sign bearing his name in Asnières. Today's chefs contribute to the prestige and appeal of the towns where they operate. JEANELLE /*Paris-Match*

26. Joël Robuchon, the most inventive and most modest of our French cooks at the moment. MAYUMI TOZUKA

Brive
Aurillac
Lot
Capdenac
Villeneuve d'Aveyron
Cahors
Rodez
Villefranche de Rouergue
Najac
Montauban
Aveyron
Albi

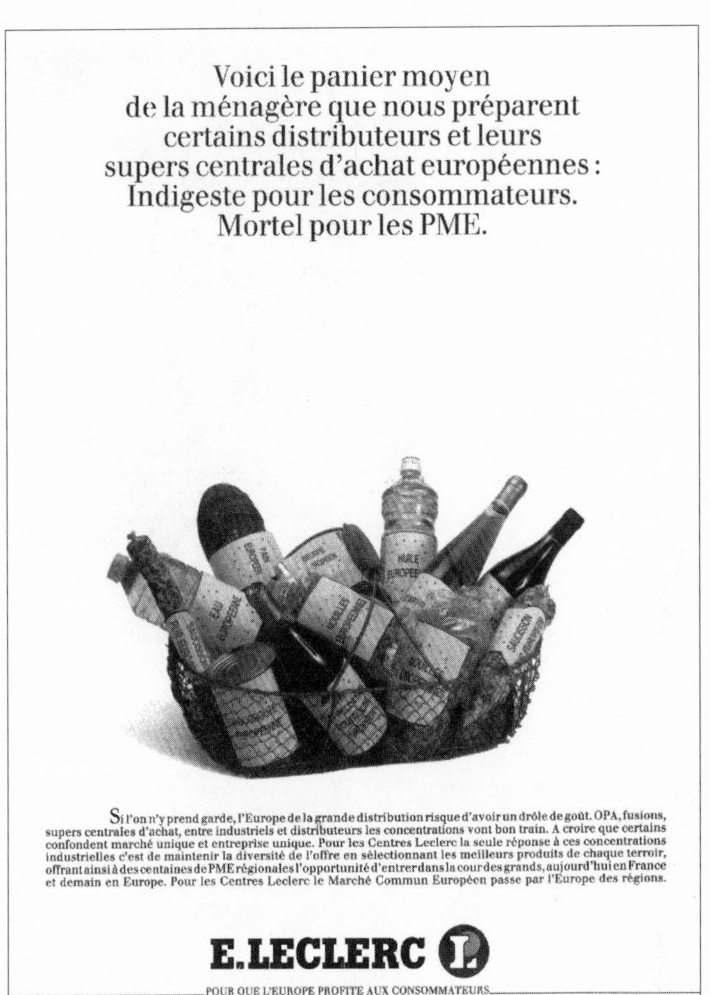

27. *Facing page top*: "The Last Supper revisited by F. G." A few of the greatest French chefs gathered around Paul Bocuse. FRANCIS GIACOBETTI/TRINQUART

28. *Facing page bottom*: A gastronomic interpretation of the tourist geography of Rouergue. DESIGN BY TOGMAN. REGIONAL TOURISM OFFICE OF VILLEFRANCHE-DE-ROUERGUE

29. The agribusiness industry and mass marketing can lead to improved taste for foods, as indicated in this manifesto by Edouard Leclerc that appeared in newspapers in May 1990.

30. Force-feeding a goose. There will always be a place for quality artisanal products, such as foie gras. X.D.R.

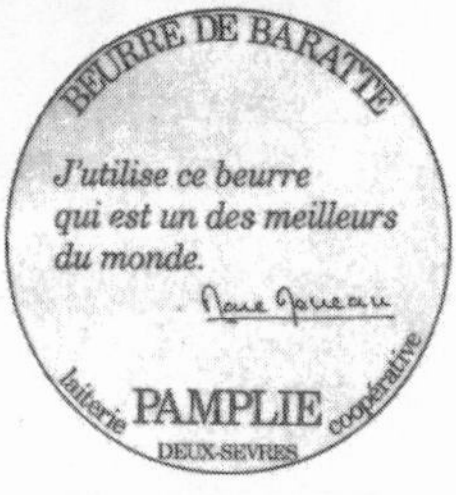

31. The great chefs are a driving force behind quality food products. Marc Merreau (L'Espérance, in Saint-Père-sous-Vézelay) attests to that on the packaging for Deux-Sèvres butter.

32. The future of quality food products, rooted in specific regions and not in generic, high-yield agribusiness.

33. Jacques Puisais, cofounder of the French Institute of Taste, during an educational session on the senses in a primary school. BERNARD AND CATHERINE DESJEUX

Chapter Four

The Gastronomic Restaurant, or *Haute Cuisine* on the Streets

THE WORLDWIDE SUCCESS of the word "restaurant" gives the French good cause for pride. First used to designate a rich and fortifying bouillon, and then various little stimulating dishes suitable for restoring failing health, or quite simply energy depleted by fatigue and hunger, by the end of the eighteenth century it no longer applied to anything but that establishment where they were served. The seminal event for this institution took place in 1765, on the rue des Poulies, near the Louvre, where a certain Boulanger, called Champ d'Oiseaux, served "restaurants," that is, broths, but also portions of sheep's trotters in a white sauce under the Latin insignia for cooking: *Venite ad me, omnes qui stomacho laboratis, et ego vos restaurabo*. His activity earned him a lawsuit on the part of the caterers[1] (indeed, they had a monopoly on the selling of cooked meats), but he won his case, thus assuring his profession a place in the sun.

Stephen Mennell has shown how archaic the institutions for

eating away from home were as they existed at that time in France, and by comparison, how modern the English ones.[2] As there were a number of cultural upheavals, the French restaurant does not have a simple genealogy. It also possesses an English ancestry. The taverns on the other side of the Channel, that is, those establishments where wine was served, thus distinguishing them from the pubs, were often elegant and renowned. During the 1670s, one of the most famous and refined of the seventeenth-century London taverns was run by the son of a president of the Bordeaux Parliament, M. de Pontac. There he served the wine produced by his father on his Haut-Brion domain.[3] In 1777, the marquis of Caraccioli wrote of English aristocrats: "Poorly housed, except in their country estates, they have no better cooking than in the taverns. That is where they often take a stranger to meet their friends. . . . Is that where a lord lives?"[4] This last remark provides another key to understanding the belated development of counterparts to the English tavern in France: at the end of the *ancien régime*, anyone who truly possessed gastronomic tastes had at his disposal a talented cook and a brigade of kitchen boys to serve him. That was the result of Louis XIV's policy for attracting a whole segment of the nobility to his court and into his Parisian entourage.

The celebrated Boulanger affair is an indication of aspirations toward a new style but also of the decline of the guild system. Very quickly, a few restaurants opened in Paris during the reign of Louis XIV. They surpassed the caterers in prestige and even acquired a national and international reputation. As Diderot wrote in a letter to Sophie Volland, "I left there to go dine at the restaurant on the rue des Poulies; one is treated well there, but at a high price."[5] Unlike at the caterers', where customers could seat themselves at the single guest table—as was still true not long ago in certain Italian *trattorie* in the country or in Greek taverns—restaurant owners seated their clients at little tables covered with tablecloths. The latter thus escaped the crowds and could hold confidential or romantic conversations. They were served individual portions of dishes they chose from a framed sheet of paper, before settling up the "payment card," that is, the check.

Antoine Beauvilliers praises the profession to the skies. He is also an essential link in a historical geography of French gastronomy, because he was one of the first provisions officers of a prince—the count of Provence, the future Louis XVIII—to establish himself on his own. There was Clause à Strasbourg before him, but he had only one specialty, pâté de foie gras. As for Beauvilliers, he opened a chic restaurant where the Paris smart set flocked and allowed the *haute cuisine* of the court to descend into the streets. He first established himself at 26 rue de Richelieu, under the sign of La Grande Taverne de Londres, and then two steps away, but at the heart of fashionable Paris, under the gallery of Valois at the Palais-Royal. "An elegant salon, the waiters nicely attired, a carefully maintained cellar and superior cuisine," Brillat-Savarin would say.[6] In short, a mixture of the best to be found in the houses of nobility, at good caterers, and in the cafés, the first of which belonged to the Neapolitan Francesco Capelli, called Procope, and opened in 1674 on the rue de Tournon, before it moved, in 1684, to the rue de l'Ancienne-Comédie where it still exists, its elegant décor restored. In about the same period, the Provençal restaurant Les Trois Frères was established in the neighborhood, serving bouillabaisse and *brandade de morue*. Even if we may imagine that the Provençal cuisine at this establishment lost some of its local color under the Paris sky, it still represented a minor revolution. Culinary exoticism earned acclaim, and to eat in a restaurant implied the acceptance—or the pursuit—of a certain change of scenery. This is still true today, even while the most famous cooks on the planet, Bocuse, Chapel, and a few others, come (or rather, *came*, since the death of the poet of Mionnay) to chow down at the bistro d'Odette à la Part-Dieu of Lyons, on monkfish with tomatoes on rice and goat cheese accompanied by white Mâcon, after having gone to market.[7] The Formica and the forks, their four tines no longer parallel, offer these masters a rest from their impeccable houses, as they are forever hungry for reassuring moments of frank camaraderie around dishes they can eat without a fuss.

One Revolution Can Hide Another

The proliferation of quality restaurants in Paris dates from the Revolution. It is true, as has often been said, that a certain number of talented cooks thus lost their masters, through emigration or the guillotine. That is the case with Méot, cook for the prince of Condé, who established himself on the rue de Valois in 1791. But the other reason involves the clientele, that is, the heads of the Revolution themselves. They decided to abolish all symbols of the *ancien régime* and religion but wisely resolved not to throw the baby away with the bath water. Of all the cultural and artistic edifices constructed by the monarchy and the court, gastronomy was the one easiest to rehabilitate, and no one would ever suspect Marat or Danton of being enemies of the Republic because they went to dine lavishly at Méot's. Destroying statues or guillotining the royal family did not stand in the way of enjoying truffles; on the contrary, it was a people's victory, by which their representatives should rightfully profit! The provincial representatives present in Paris throughout the Revolution, who lodged in the boarding houses, provided a large and stable enough clientele to allow restaurants to proliferate. Far from doing harm, the competition was good for business, a common phenomenon even today in commercial geography whenever it is a matter of anomalous, that is, rare, goods and services. Consider, for example, the jewelry shops on la place Vendôme or the specialty food boutiques on la place de la Madeleine. The same link between taverns and parliamentary life has long been observed in London.[8] Thus, descending from its pedestal, French *haute cuisine* remained very tied to the exercise of political power, just as it had under the *ancien régime*.

In 1798, Sébastien Mercier amusingly recounts the fortunes of the lavatory keeper at the Palais-Egalité:

> That one was very judicious who, seeing the restaurant owners and ice cream makers establishing their dining halls and their private rooms at what had been the Royal Palace in as great a number and as close together as bees in a hive, had lavatories constructed for the diners at 18 *livres* a head. He thought that so much truffled turkey, so much salmon, so much Mayence ham, so much boar's head, so much Bologne sausage, so much pâté, so much wine, liquor, sorbet, ice cream and lemonade ought to find there, in the last analysis, a common reservoir, and that, by making it spacious and especially convenient enough for so many people who make everything into a matter of sensual pleasure, the *caput mortuum* of the surrounding kitchens would become a gold mine for him.[9]

The emperor Vespasien himself no doubt thought that having lavatories close to eating and drinking places could ensure substantial revenues!

A few years later, in 1803, in the first issue of the *Almanach des gourmands*, Grimod de La Reynière describes how the Palais-Royal had become a mecca for quality restuarants (see map 3):

> That is how one after another the Méots, the Roberts, the Rozes, the Vérys, the Lédas, the Brigauts, the Legacques, the Beauvilliers, the Naudets, the Taulliers, the Nicoles, etc. were established, nearly millionaires today. Before 1789, there were not more than a hundred. . . . Now there are maybe five or six times more.[10]

We can count 3,000 of them under the Restoration, of all types, from the most refined to the simplest, meant for students.[11] And Grimod adds in 1804:

> The heart of most wealthy Parisians has suddenly metamorphosed into a gizzard. . . . Also there is no city in the world where there are so many merchants and makers of foods. You can count a hundred restaurants in Paris for every bookstore.

That proportion has hardly changed, even in the Latin Quarter. . . .

The craze for these new establishments was so great that some of the most luxurious cafés were transformed into restaurants. Among them, the café de Chartres became Le Grand-Véfour, the only evidence left today of the Palais-Royal's glorious gastronomic past.

Under the Empire, a new distribution emerged (see map 3). The Palais-Royal no longer had a monopoly; establishments were opened in the Halles Quarter (Le Rocher de Cancale, rue Montorgueil) and already along the great boulevards (du Tem-

THE PALAIS-ROYAL RESTAURANTS AND CAFÉS
(at the end of the eighteenth century and under the Empire)

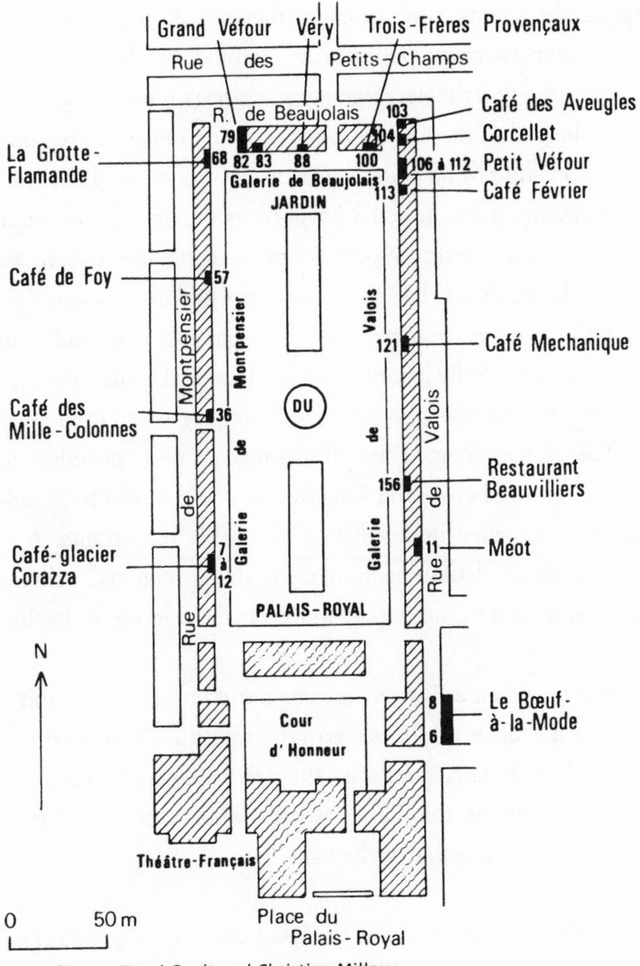

According to Henri Gault and Christian Millau, *Guide Gourmand de la France* (Paris: Hachette, 1970).

ple, des Italiens). One all by itself in the west, Ledoyen, prefigured the success of the Champs-Elysées Quarter. At the Palais-Royal, the clients came to enjoy themselves, but their workplaces were nearby; henceforth it would be the areas with promenades and theaters that attracted restaurants.

At the end of the Empire, gastronomic France had regained all the prestige of its court *haute cuisine*, thanks to Talleyrand and Carême, but it added a jewel to its crown: the restaurant where the fare could be just as fine, but the atmosphere was more relaxed than it had been under the gilded wainscoting of the crumbling *ancien régime*. With the passing years and as the new masters of the country merged with the old ones, the supreme elegance of the eighteenth century reemerged. With the fall of Napoléon, when all of Europe's elite, nostalgic for French culture before the Revolution, could return to breathe the Paris air, they invaded the fashionable restaurants. A bit later, Eugène Briffaut summarized the foreigners' relief at rediscovering a France equal, indeed even superior, to itself:

> In 1814, when a Europe at arms hurled itself as one unit against France, all the heads of this multitude had but one cry: Paris! And, in Paris, they demanded the Palais-Royal, and at the Palais-Royal, what was their first desire? To be seated at the table.[12]

For the most part, it was the head cooks of the restaurants who seized the monopoly on gastronomic creativity. Outside of the royal and then the imperial court, and the palace of the Republic, only a few of the wealthiest upper middle-class families reorganized the household staffs required of nobility during the *ancien régime*. And having a domestic brigade did not stop them from eating at restaurants, which offered a change of scenery and where human relationships are not the same as at home. That is particularly true in the case of men's relationships with the opposite sex, because it was improper, until the end of the nineteenth century, to go out to restaurants in the company of one's spouse . . . which explains the success of the *salons particuliers*. Those of Lapérouse were famous for their bidets hidden under the seats and for their mirrors covered with lines traced by the *demi-mondaines*, thus verifying the authenticity of the diamonds offered by their patrons. Only the mirrors have survived in this beautiful house, now listed on the historic register!

Chefs who worked "in wealthy houses" quite often switched over to restaurants, once they had learned their art and earned a certain reputation. The inverse was much more rare. In-house work was indeed much more peaceful but less stimulating than restaurant work. There you satisfied the tastes and the fancies of a single master, whereas in the restaurant, there were dozens of regular customers who had to be pleased enough to come back. The career of Adolphe Dugléré is one model.[13] Born in 1805, he worked at the home of the Baron de Rothschild until 1848, where he benefited from the teachings of Antonin Carême. He then directed the Provençal kitchens of the Trois Frères, and then, at the age of sixty-two, crowned his career at the Café Anglais beginning in 1867. The International Exposition earned this establishment, and a few others, an international reputation that owed much to Dugléré. In return, he won recognition he would never have obtained otherwise, especially because he never published a book. The most famous recipes in his register resulted from a publicity exchange with the establishment's best clients, who belonged to the worlds of fashion, art, finance, and politics: *pommes Anna* was dedicated to Anna Deslions, the prostitute; *potage Germiny* to the Count of Germiny, officer of the Banque de France; *poularde Albufera* to Marshall Suchet, duke of Albufera—this was a recipe that Carême had dedicated to him; and, not to forget himself, *barbue Dugléré*. No chef today would dare dedicate a dish to himself, despite the temptation probably felt by some of them. On the other hand, even if the custom is a bit out of date, some dishes are always associated with the names of the world's rich and powerful: not long ago, Raymond Oliver created a *pigeon Rainier III*, Bocuse a *soupe de truffes VGE*; and La Tour d'Argent menu is still sprinkled with such names. The link uniting gastronomy to power is a constant.

The Geography of French Gastronomy in the Nineteenth Century

Throughout the first half of the nineteenth century, gastronomic creation remained essentially Parisian. Some restaurants were opened in big cities, but few names were passed on to posterity before the twentieth century. One ate well in the provinces, straightforward, generous food, prepared with local products and rather inexpensive, but not extravagant. In Lyons, for example, discreet, well-to-do establishments proliferated for the silk merchants and the magistrates, bistros for the artisans.[14] Grimod de La Reynière seems to have appreciated Marseilles restaurants around 1810, documenting promise that was hardly fulfilled as the century advanced: "Marseilles is a most agreeable city to stay in. The artist, the man of letters, the merchant, the pleasure seeker, the gourmet, and the sensualist can each find something to satisfy himself."[15] The Phocaean capital would have to wait for the end of the twentieth century to regain a little gastronomic luster. In the 1956 *Michelin Guide*, the city and its surroundings still boasted only one two-star restaurant and only five one-star restaurants, while the Lyons area counted one three-star, six two-star, and twelve one-star. Even if Marseilles has made progress, the report remains similar today.

In Paris, in contrast, the gastronomic restaurant business is a field as creative and fluctuating as the fashion industry, theater, or music. This makes sense, since it exists thanks to the upper middle classes who hold the purse strings and dictate their tastes to all the cooks, who get even by presenting them, as Beauvilliers had begun to do, with astronomical tabs. Both the client and the restaurant owner desire ostentation and a steady increase in the number as well as the rarity of dishes and wines presented on the menu. The recently deceased essayist, Jean-Paul Aron, strongly emphasizes the insatiable appetite of the *nouveaux riches* *16* and perhaps does not emphasize enough the sense of frank pleasure such an appetite also implies. The pot-bellied middle-class man wearing a watch chain and eating supper at the Café Riche in the company of a dancer is not only a exhibitionist in terms of his wealth. He is also a man who knows how to appreciate the finer things and who has the leisure time at his disposal to take advantage of them. His pleasure is greater still if he has gone through hard times to get there. To be more precise, his pleasure compares to the peasant's, whose ordinary fare remains meager, who lives it up for three days during a wedding celebration, thus overcoming a certain number of material and moral barriers that normally limit his horizons. Although analogous in terms of consumption, the pleasure experienced by the bourgeoisie is different from that felt by the eighteenth-century nobles who drowned their idleness in romantic little suppers, enervating themselves with pleasures but never achieving bliss. If he is not a prodigal son, the *nouveau riche* spends money he has earned through his expertise, thus lending a certain optimism to his appetite, sometimes a little showy, it is true.

Balzac offers fine scenes of the Parisian restaurant life of his period. The restaurants he mentions most often are, first, the Rocher de Cancale, rue Montorgueil; and then the Cadran Bleu, boulevard du Temple; the Café Anglais,[18] the Café Riche, the Café de Paris, all three on the boulevard des Italiens; and Le Boeuf à la Mode, at the Palais-Royal, already on the decline. Thus, this was the great epoch of the boulevard, but fashions ran more and more to the west, abandoning the boulevard du Temple and then the boulevard des Italiens itself to spread out toward the end of the century between the Chaussée d'Antin and the Madeleine (see map 4). "The real Paris is a strip of asphalt trimmed with puny shrubs, corseted with iron, that stretches from the Opéra-Comique to the rue Royale. . . . Beyond that, there are the suburbs, the Odéonies, distant, unknown things," notes Maurice Guillemot in 1901.[19] And in 1902, Gaston Jollivet writes in *Le Gaulois*:

> The disappearance of the Maison Dorée restaurant, coming after that of the Café Riche: is this evidence that Paris is getting tired of paying high prices for its restaurant meals? I hardly think so, watching the continuous wave of more and more great "cabarets." The truth is that if the Maison Dorée, after the Café Riche, and also the Brébant, closes its doors, it is because it was located on that poor boulevard now so out of fashion. Indeed a luxury establishment must have doubly solid financial backing to resist the tide that more and more pushes the fashionable movement beyond the Madeleine and the Rond-Point, to the "far west" of the avenue du Bois and du Bois itself.[20]

This is the rage of Ledoyen, the Pavillon Elysée, Laurant, the Champs-Elysées, the Pré Catelan, the Pavillon d'Armenonville, the Madrid, and the Grande Cascade au Bois de Boulogne. The Left Bank also awoke to gastronomy, while the success of the little soup restaurants frequented by students and artists persisted. The Café d'Harcourt, the Tour d'Argent, Lapérouse, and Foyot acquired reputations comparable to those of establishments on the Right Bank.

Throughout the twentieth century, this distribution endured. Some expansion took place into the districts surrounding the capital and the suburbs, but 90 percent of the establishments were located to the west of a gare de l'Est–Bastille–porte d'Orléans line.

Gastronomy and the Beginning of Tourism

The French and foreign middle classes who had gotten used to eating well in Paris restaurants were very interested in finding fare of similar quality in all the European luxury hotels where business or leisure drew them. Thus, prestigious hotels were opened for this wealthy and demanding clientele, also more mobile thanks to the railroad, in economic capitals, at seaside or mountain health resorts, and finally at thermal spas, where they went to take the waters as well as to treat themselves to a good time.

The historical geography of the luxury hotels echoes that of the restaurants: English precursors, French development. The first hotels, similar to aristocratic residences—that is, luxury establishments where you could take rooms and be served fine meals—were English, and opened in the 1820s in London, around Saint James's Street and Piccadilly.[21] The Saint James Hotel, the most famous of these, was run by an English student of Carême's, Francatelli. Beginning in the 1880s, huge and luxurious hotels—so luxurious that they were called *palaces*—

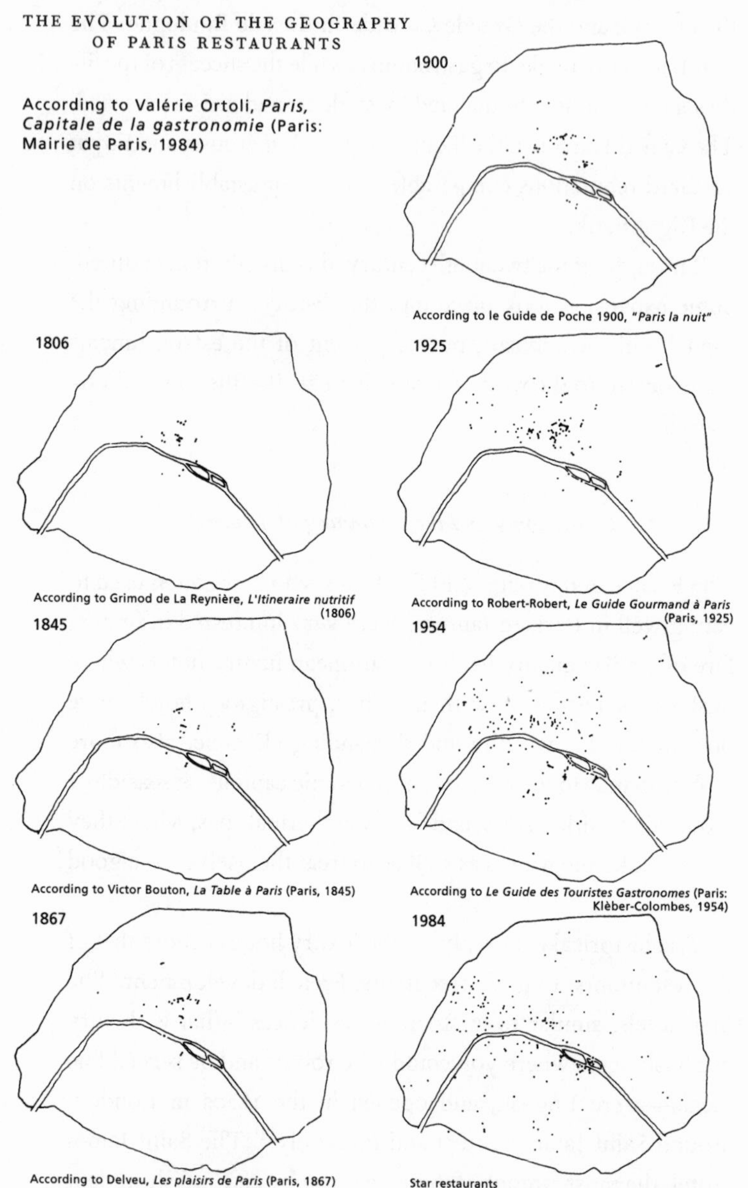

According to le Guide de Poche 1900, *"Paris la nuit"*

According to Grimod de La Reynière, *L'Itineraire nutritif* (1806)

According to Robert-Robert, *Le Guide Gourmand à Paris* (Paris, 1925)

According to Victor Bouton, *La Table à Paris* (Paris, 1845)

According to *Le Guide des Touristes Gastronomes* (Paris: Klèber-Colombes, 1954)

According to Delveu, *Les plaisirs de Paris* (Paris, 1867)

Star restaurants
according to the *Bottin gourmand* (Paris: Didot Bottin, 1984)

opened in London, Baden-Baden, Paris, Touquet, Trouville, Deauville, Cabourg, along the Riviera, etc. Many of them were started and run by Frenchmen. Baden-Baden was an enclave of French culture in Germany, superbly orchestrated by Jacques Bénazet.

But the most famous of these Frenchmen, good managers and admirable creators of luxury and sensual delight at the same time, were César Ritz and Auguste Escoffier. To the first—who was originally Swiss, but spent his life defending the French colors—fell the care of the hotel; to the second, the care of the restaurant. After meeting up at the Grand Hôtel of Monte-Carlo, the two of them turned the Savoy of London into one of the hot spots of Europe. You could eat there wonderfully well, and soon modern kitchens, organized into several parts as Escoffier advocated, became the model. Then came the Ritz in Paris, on la place Vendôme; then the Carlton of London and many other luxury hotels where both were called in as advisors.

With no modesty—the expansive and affectionate vanity of certain great chefs is one of their charms—Escoffier himself describes his methods and his influence in a passage of great geographic and economic relevance from his memoirs:[22]

> The art of cooking may be one of the most useful forms of diplomacy. Called to every part of the world to organize the restaurant services of the most lavish hotels, I have always been careful to require French materials, French products,[23] and above all, French personnel. Because the development of French cooking is largely due to thousands of French cooks who work in all four corners of the world. They have expatriated to make known, even in the most remote countries, French products and the art of

> preparing them. It is a great satisfaction for me to have contributed to this development. Throughout my entire career, I have "sown" some two thousand cooks all over the world. Most of them have founded lines in these countries, and you could say that they are so many grains of wheat sown in uncultivated territories. Today, France harvests the bounty.

Moreover, Escoffier published prolifically. In his *Guide culinaire* (*Culinary Guide*), appearing in 1901 and widely translated, he simplified menus, recipes, and especially presentations. The pedestals and elaborate centerpieces were eliminated, carving in the dining room began to lose its hold, and menus *à prix fixe* were recommended over those interminable *à la carte* lists of promises impossible to keep. Prosper Montagné would go still further in *La Grande Cuisine illustrée* (*The Grand Cuisine Illustrated*), which he published with Salles in 1900. Escoffier's influence over Europe culminated with the "Epicurean dinner" he prepared in London's Cecil Hotel, which was served simultaneously to hundreds of guests in thirty-seven cities throughout Europe![24] This internationalism would gradually go awry. After World War II, the luxury hotels were no longer what they had been. Often they served a bland menu with very distant French tones, so-called "international" cuisine. But after a long eclipse, in the last ten years or so, inspiration has once again returned to the great luxury hotels in Paris, Nice, Monte Carlo, and Tokyo, which house a few of the planet's excellent French restaurants.

In order for the quality of luxury hotel cuisine to remain consistent from one end of France to the other, indeed throughout Europe, entire kitchen brigades were readily dispatched according to the seasonal migrations of the bourgeoisie. Jean Ducloux, of the Greuze restaurant in Tournus, describes these astonishing migrations from Paris to Le Touquet in the 1920s:

> In the summer at l'Ermitage du Touquet, the management amassed three hundred service personnel to satisfy its upper middle-class clients during the two-week height of the season. The working classes arrived from Paris on a sort of pleasure train. The eighty cooks, assistants, and kitchen boys hired to constitute the brigade all met up again on one or two reserved cars. As other brigades embarked the same day to go populate other still-empty hotels, there was a long train of cooks leaving from the Saint-Lazare station. And during the bumpy journey, which then lasted a long time, the guild spirit that the big city had dissolved was reborn among the cooks.[25]

Until about 1925, the clients of these hotels also used public transportation, but under entirely different conditions than common mortals. The farmer or modest city dweller drew a meal from his sack, thus permeating the second- and third-class compartments with powerful local odors. During this time, the middle-class gourmand had lunch at the station's gastronomic buffet before boarding the train. At Arcachon, he enjoyed local dishes in an amazing Chinese pagoda. At Dijon, he ate better than in many Parisian restaurants.[26] At the Lyons station's Train Bleu, which dates from 1901, the astounding decor was a foretaste of the marvels awaiting on the Riviera. Moreover, the Paris smart set was called upon to perfect the illusion, since Sarah Bernhardt herself was represented in one of the frescoes. . . . Little has changed today, and stars of all kinds graciously help promote Saint-Tropez, Cannes, and

Deauville, where restaurant owners know how to take advantage of this. . . .

In the train, it was possible to take one's meals in the dining car—an American invention by Pullman—beginning from 1883 on the lines leaving Paris for Normandy, and then on the Orient-Express, thanks to the Compagnie des Wagons-lits. On the Constantinople line, the luxurious decor, elaborate table, and extravagant dishes were unprecedented. In 1900, the company had two hundred dining cars at its disposal, distributed among all the great European railway lines.[27] Naturally, for the most part, French food was served. Today, in total decline, railway restaurants are attempting to find new inspiration which, for the time being, is hardly gastronomic, with a few rare exceptions. Finally, let us mention the sumptuous fare served on ocean liners. Forced into idleness by the voyage, the clientele paid even more attention to it there than in restaurants on land.

"On est heureux, Nationale 7"

As early as the end of World War I, the automobile dethroned the forms of travel gastronomy born with the railway, just as the airplane would after World War II. This was a windfall for the old coaching and country inns that only survived thanks to weddings and banquets and business travelers. Actually, the phenomenon did not spread throughout France very quickly. For a long time, the privileged axis was the one connecting France's three great metropolises and terminating in Nice. The RN 6 and the RN 7 became long chains of gastronomic inns where wealthy tourists with automobiles stopped when going on vacation.

These stops were soon suggested by the guides edited by

Michelin. Moreover, the "Bibendum," mascot of the famous tire maker and developed from a idea of the "prince of the gastronomes," Curnonsky, marked a new alliance between the automobile and eating well. "On est heureux, Nationale 7" (One is happy on Route 7), sang Charles Trenet in the 1950s: indeed, when one ate lunch at Dumaine's at Saulieu or at Hure's in Avallon, when one dined at Mère Brazier's in Lyons or in her chalet in the Luère pass, or at Fernand Point's in Vienne, before plunging into the exoticism of Mediterranean cuisine at Thuillier's in Baux-de-Provence and taking up winter or summer quarters at Baudouin's in Antibes or at one of the many coastal hotels only open at first from October to May, and then, after 1931, in summer as well! In winter, after returning to Megève or Chamonix, one stopped at Bise's in Talloires. This line-up of good restaurants constituted the total list of Michelin's provincial "three stars" in the 1956 edition of the *Guide*. As for the capital, it counted four of them: Le Grand-Véfour (Oliver), Maxim's (Vaudable), La Tour d'Argent (Terrail) and Lapérouse (Topolinski).

For the thrill of driving fast and the pleasure of eating well, the arts and entertainment smart set of Paris descended upon "*la Côte*" in automobiles and contributed to the reputations of the establishments where they stopped. Their guest books are collections of the most prestigious signatures on the planet, from Maurice Chevalier to the queen of England. Jean Cocteau was one of the most faithful regulars on this pleasure route where a rush of madness returns with the lovely weather.

Beyond the royal axis, things changed gradually. Provincial inns and hotels got used to receiving guests who were passing through and wanted to sample local specialties. One meal improvised for two Parisian motorists by the owner of a small Sousceyrac hotel provided Pierre Benoît with the starting point for a lovely novel in 1931.[28] The lunch was far from Spartan and in no way resembled the international cuisine of luxury hotels. The hostess, who claimed she was totally destitute, managed to serve a snack consisting of foie gras, crayfish, trout caught the night before, stuffed wild mushrooms, jugged hare, and a roasted chicken! The two clients, who belonged to the wealthy middle class, could not praise their meal enough. This was symptomatic of a new phenomenon: the interest in regionalism so fundamental to one of the facets of present-day gastronomy.

Moreover, for a long time in the provinces, regional dishes would cost less than the grand cuisine in the style of Escoffier, reserved for the luxury hotels. It was these everyday dishes, inherited from country holiday cooking and prepared by the innkeepers, that middle-class tourists discovered on their vacations at the time when paid holidays were developing and then becoming general practice. Generally from large cities, the tourists took wild pleasure in the change of scenery offered through local cuisines and wines consumed in the landscapes of their origin. Pagnol echoes this in *Cigalon*: "Wretched shame! No restaurant? Let's see, Chalumeau, what good is this country if it hasn't spawned a single, or even several, restaurants? There's no justification for such a landscape."[29] We must add that, for a long time, the prices at these establishments remained modest for the remarkable amount and careful preparation of the food, and this was true throughout the country, except in those resorts long devoted to luxury. This contrast to Parisian prices, which made modest purses happy, was a consequence of the economic and cultural isolation of many rural regions. Such isolation is rare today, but you still eat for less off the beaten paths. In its 1980 edition, the *Gault-Millau Guide* praises the Auberge de Chavannes à Courlans, in the Jura Mountains, for "its very reasonable prices and its 75-franc menu, superb quality for the price. It is true," it adds, "that Courlans is not just next door."

And Afterward, You Talk About It!

Before considering the contemporary aspects of this movement to democratize *haute cuisine* that began with the Revolution, we must consider the talk that accompanied it. It has been said that French people of all social classes like to talk about what they eat and drink, before, during, and after, with the exception of certain prudish circles who follow the Anglo-Saxon rules of polite behavior. The famous, "And afterward, you talk about it" is a line attributed to many fine eaters. According to Maurice Lelong, it comes from Balzac, who used it on one of his guests, ready to bolt down a great wine that just been poured for him:

> "That wine, my friend, you regard lovingly."
> "And after that?"
> "After that, you breathe it in."
> "And after that?"
> "You set it back down on the table, untouched, with pious devotion."
> "And after that?"
> "After that, you talk about it."[30]

And Maurice Lelong adds:

> Because, if it is appropriate to remain hushed before a painting, or even more so after a piece of music, the exegesis of a bottle of wine, if it is intelligent, enhances the tasting in a special way and distinguishes those inattentive drinkers from the ones who know what it is that fills their glasses.

Maybe more in France than elsewhere, the oral and written culture of fine eating and good wine runs parallel to its subject historically and supports the latter's development, in everything from popular song to learned poetry, criticism to philosophy. The gastronomic and oenological literature in French deserves its own anthology, which would require research into all branches of knowledge and poetic sensibility. One of the most developed of its facets, criticism, is essential for understanding how gastronomy was appropriated by the bourgeoisie and then by all, or nearly all, of French society. If probably more than three quarters of French adults know the name of Paul Bocuse—while many would be incapable of citing a single academician—that is the result of this descent of gastronomic criticism into the public arena.

As a literary genre, it goes back to Grimod de La Reynière. Son of a farmer general, favored by fortune but ill-favored by nature—he had webbed fingers—there was about him a deep contempt for his contemporaries, especially if they were not gourmet enough for his liking. He organized productions in sometimes doubtful taste around banquets that he gave and surrounded himself with a circle of hand-picked friends, with whom he carefully examined all that was claimed to be delectable in and around Paris. From 1803 to 1812, he published *L'Almanach des gourmands*, written with a finesse mixed with sarcasm that prefigured the style of certain contemporary critics. He brought together tasting juries who gave or denied their blessing to the various dishes provided by restaurant owners, caterers, delicatessens, pastry cooks, confectioners, etc. The results of these meticulous experiments were published in the *Almananch*, as the results of all sorts of taste trials are published in various magazines today. Though capable of arrogance and pettiness, Grimod was profoundly innovative; his ideas were taken up again and reformulated by other authors throughout the nineteenth century and into our own time. Under the *ancien régime*, the dishes and wines of quality were the result of the direct relationship between that world's rich and powerful and the producers, or sometimes the commercial intermediaries. Grimod introduced a third power, that of the critic, who sought to guide both of them and whose role would only become greater, sometimes to the point of leaving both consumers and producers dumbfounded. This is a common phenomenon: we know how the fashionable pacesetters can sometimes remake the world in their image.

Specialists in the history of gastronomy generally consider Berchoux and Brillat-Savarin to be not very talented followers, indeed even semiplagiarists, of Grimod de La Reynière. That is an injustice, because both of them, and especially Brillat-Savarin, brought back to life the old Gallic spirit and elegantly dressed it up. For them, gastronomy was, above all, an art of living happily. Both chuckled quietly as they spouted their sententious aphorisms. Grimod seems more subtle; in fact, he was perpetually unsatisfied, disguising under a clever pen profound self-contempt and no less profound discontent with the world, even in a cloud of the strongest aroma of truffles. He is comparable in his own domain to what Rousseau, Sade, or Casanova were elsewhere. Basically, Grimod was the theorist for the precious art of gourmet eating at the end of the *ancien régime* as Berchoux and Brillat-Savarin were for the nineteenth-century middle class. Their contemporary heir would be James de Coquet.

In the nineteenth century, gastronomic criticism was illustrated by a great many authors. We will mention Charles Monselet, the very well-known journalist of the Second Empire, who developed the "*chronique de table*" genre. He founded a short-lived review, *Le Gourmet*, and also published many works on his favorite theme, among them *La Cuisinière pratique* (*The*

Practical Cook). Like Brillat-Savarin before him and like his contemporaries, Baron Brisse or Léon de Fos, Monselet was a bachelor. This is not completely a matter of chance, and without going too far, and so avoiding the pitfall of cheap Freudianism, we can relate this trait to the Catholic—secular or regular—clergy's interest in eating well that we have already mentioned. Many of the gourmets scattered throughout nineteenth- and twentieth-century literature are also bachelors, at least at the beginning of the works. That is the case with Erckmann-Chatrian's Ami Fritz,[31] Paul de Courselles and Sixte Delorme's Oncle Mistral,[32] and Marcel Rouff's Dodin-Bouffant.[33]

The most famous in this cohort of bachelor "culinographers"—to borrow a word from Prosper Montagné, who had little love for the critics despite what they contributed to his reputation[34]—is Maurice Sailland, known as Curnonsky (*cur non* sky; why not sky? This is the epoch of the Stavisky affair).[35] Journalist and writer, he owed his pseudonym to Alphonse Allais and sharpened his pen by serving as assistant to Willy. Even more than Monselet, he made a career of his gourmet tastes, but also of his taste for travel. After World War I, he traveled up and down France for many years in the company of Marcel Rouff, with whom he published twenty-eight volumes entitled *La France gastronomique* (*Gastronomic France*). Marcel Rouff's death interrupted this tour of France, only incomplete by four volumes. Of all the tourist guides appearing since the nineteenth century, this was the first to be expressly devoted to good regional dishes, good wines, and good restaurants. The influence of this work was immense. Henceforth, right beside Parisian *haute cuisine*, there would be a place of honor for the ultimate in regional cooking. Foreigners and the French never forgot it and would make eating well one of the driving forces of tourism in France. Curnonsky's consecration came in 1927.

Paris-Soir organized a referendum among its readers to elect the "prince of the gastronomes." Out of 3,388 votes, "Cur" received 1,823, as opposed to 1,037 for Maurice des Ombliaux, the other votes being divided among Camille Cerf, Léon Daudet, Alib Bab, Pomiane, etc. In the wake of this victory, Curnonsky founded the Académie des gastronomes, an institution that came to be added to the many clubs and brotherhoods devoted to good eating and good wines. Beginning in 1947, he took part in the success of a periodical with quite a large readership, *Cuisine et Vins de France*. Until his death in 1956, he never stopped writing or traveling. Honors and invitations were heaped upon him, including one from President Doumergue. And he was feared by food service figures and restaurant owners whose fame and fortune he could establish. Here we have two examples among a thousand. One day, sampling a tart from the demoiselles Tatin at Lamotte-Beuvron, he was delighted and made both the pastry and the establishment famous throughout France;[36] today, it is one of the best-known French desserts. In 1922, discovering that Mélanie Rouat, a village grocer and dry goods merchant in Riec-sur-Belon, cooked amazingly well, he convinced her to open a restaurant. A few years later, it was one of Brittany's most renowned eating places.

Curnonsky's judgments were irrevocable; his comments could sometimes be scathing, but in general he only used his verbal facilities or his pen for jovial compliments, the image of his princely reputation. But most of all, he displayed a wild pleasure in the actor's life that his fame imposed upon him. His role in shaping the gastronomic geography of France as it emerged with the inception of automobile tourism served as a supplement to the guides.

Throughout the nineteenth century, guides appeared in France: travel guides, guides for eating out, for the gourmand, for the pleasure seeker, etc. Most of them were devoted to the capital.[37] The Joanne guides or those of the German Karl Baedecker gave information on the food and lodging the tourist could hope to find in the provinces but left the gastronome unsatisfied. Not until the automobile boom would the situation improve. André Michelin's guide appeared beginning in 1900: it included numerous addresses of hotels, restaurants, and garages, but no indication of the quality of the fare. Distinguishing better restaurants with a star began with the 1926 edition; the 1931 edition established a hierarchy going from one star to three. Then came mention of the three best specialties and recommended wines. With print runs today of more than a million copies, the *Michelin Guide* remains the most highly respected and appreciated by professionals as well as by gourmets, despite criticisms from certain journalists and restaurant owners. Its annual publication and its verdicts are eagerly awaited and made the subject of a great many commentaries. The complex organization its production requires, the strict anonymity, and the absence of advertising presuppose the kind of major investment only a huge enterprise can afford. But the success of the formula also rests upon a very large following among the population. One out of fifty people in France buy it; probably more than one out of five read it or use it from time to time, if only for daydreaming. *Haute cuisine* is less and less the privilege of the ruling classes, fully justifying Brillat-Savarin's claim:

> Gourmandism is one of the principle bonds in society; it is what gradually expands that spirit of conviviality uniting the various social strata every day, what forms them into a single whole, animates conversation, and smoothes the rough edges of conventional inequality.[38]

After World War II, the frenzy to forget the lean years and the prosperity of the Glorious Thirties precipitated this general movement of heightened interest in fine cuisine. Once again, the French were willing to spend money for nothing so readily as for eating well. Most of the daily newspapers and reviews began running a food column, which readers followed attentively. Gaz de France and manufacturers of stoves—called "*cuisinières*"—like Arthur-Martin organized courses in the neighborhood cinemas, given by good chefs and meant for the mothers of local families. Those who wished to could thus add to the recipes they inherited from their mothers and grandmothers.

And then came television, which, in 1953, asked Raymond Oliver to host, with the star hostess Catherine Langeais, a practical program entitled *Art et magie de la cuisine* (*The Art and Magic of Cooking*). It met with immediate success. We must say that Oliver knew his subject and that he was not lacking in eloquence. From a family of Gironde innkeepers, he came to understand, over the course of his apprenticeship in Paris, what the capital could offer him. He knew how to make the Grand-Véfour, which he bought in 1948, into *the* fashionable restaurant. Colette, Cocteau, and many other celebrities kept their napkin rings there. In his television programs, he demonstrated an authority paired with a touch of bumptiousness that pleased viewers. He did not hesitate to modify his own regional recipes to align them with Parisian tastes. A man of culture, he was one of the most eloquent spokesmen for the culinary transformations that take place in a metropolis like Paris.

> "One day," he recounted, "Prince Pierre of Monaco asked me for a dish that could replace the traditional partridge at the height of the hunting season. What a stroke of luck, I was going to create Prince Rainier III's pigeon.

It was a good year, fresh truffles, fresh foie gras, young Armagnac. As a concession made to the bled Bresse pigeons, a Parisian cuisine was born that included a series of elements that are, in my opinion, distinctive to Parisian cooking. If we analyze this dish by breaking down the elements and techniques, we can note that the pigeon comes from Bresse, but it is bled instead of being suffocated, according to our method in the southwest. It is boned, which points, first, to my interest in Chinese cooking, and second, to the desire for maintaining the gastronome's comfort in not having to struggle with the bones. . . . The stuffing is very delicate, the white meat of the poultry, ham fat, spices, it must be almost round, like a little walnut; Perigord truffles, foie gras from Landes, Ténarèze armagnac. The adventure: it's the roasting, which must be carefully watched, and, unlike poultry on a spit, basted frequently. But isn't all Parisian cooking done by those vestal virgins, the concierges? *Boeuf miroton*, *pieds d'agneau poulette*, slow simmered ragoûts: *blanquettes* or *capilotades*. Finally, everything demanding much care and time. Paris is the crucible, and it is also the consecration."[39]

Also originally from the southwest of France, Alain Senderens says basically the same thing in different words:

I often think that if I were in the provinces, I wouldn't cook the same way. There really is a different spirit, less traditionalist, in Paris, where people are crazier. In Paris, the city of celebration, it is something of a court cuisine that we prepare. My customers expect a little madness. I have to keep trying new things.[40]

As we shall see, what is essential to "*nouvelle cuisine*" is contained in this declaration in the form of a manifesto.

Raymond Oliver serves as an important figure in the history of cooking in another capacity as well. Responsible for the catering services during the Tokyo Olympics in 1964, he was the first to build a bridge between French and Far Eastern cuisines. This was the starting point for what is called "*nouvelle cuisine*." The Japanese became infatuated with French cooking at that time, and Shizuo Tsuji founded a cooking school in Osaka where all the French chefs came to teach. During these travels, they brought back to France as many new ideas, recollections, and techniques as they had brought with them to Japan.

A Parisian Phenomenon—"Nouvelle Cuisine"

Through the career and the talents of Raymond Oliver, we can come to see how Parisian supremacy, as far as gastronomic innovation is concerned, was firmly established. In the provinces, fashions are received more reticently, arriving there tempered, subdued, carefully considered, without the excesses of youth but with all the subtleties of amicable agreements made with tradition. This is nothing new: the history of architecture, furniture, or dress before the industrial revolution follows a similar pattern, and even if we lack the documents to assess it, the same is true, no doubt, for cooking.

The first wave known as *nouvelle cuisine* arrived with the tide of May 1968. Henceforth, as everyone knows, there was nothing proletarian about this "revolution." Very much to the contrary: it pushed what remained of the proletariat closer to the bourgeoisie—without, for all that, tolling the bell for egalitarian ideologies—and it profoundly transformed the morals of the bourgeoisie, particularly in matters of sexuality and food, as these two phenomena are closely related.

At the origin of *nouvelle cuisine* we find a few chefs determined to become famous and two imaginative journalists, Henri Gault and Christian Millau. Their affair began in 1960 at *Paris-Presse*, where Gault found himself responsible for a weekend excursion and food column, on a "magazine" page edited by Millau.[41] He wanted to leave the beaten paths and wrote with a brisk, even impertinent style. He won immediate success and managed to pack restaurants that had been totally unknown the day before. Even if he claimed to distinguish himself totally from the tastes of Curnonsky and his court, it was very much Curnonsky's technique that Gault used in emphasizing his own discoveries, predilections, and special favorites rather than those very reliable, well-proven establishments usually highlighted in the *Red Guide*. His prose style addressed younger (but not necessarily less wealthy!) gourmets than those who read the *Michelin Guide*. Christian Bourgois, the literary director for Julliard, first published a collection of these columns, and then asked Gault and Millau together to compile a *Guide des restaurants et des boutiques de Paris* (*Guide to Paris Restaurants and Boutiques*). The work sold 100,000 copies, and, as they themselves said, that was "how two men, with good moral standards, became a couple."[42] A little later, their column in *Paris-Presse* became a daily feature. In March 1969, they founded a monthly publication, *Le Nouveau Guide Gault-Millau*.

Their technique was both simple and sly:

> If we were surprising, it wasn't through any desire to be surprising, but quite simply because it seemed obvious to

> us that we should rank an empty and almost unknown restaurant like Denis with Lasserre, or a grandmother's Porte-Saint-Martin bistro on the same level with a grand establishment full of velvet and leather. What authorized us to decide and to make rulings in such a categorical fashion? Let us be frank: absolutely nothing. Already back then, the word "gastronome" made us, and still makes us, jump. . . . The gastronome was invented by pedants who imagined they could make themselves be taken seriously. . . . Since that *Guide Julliard*, we have never stopped being amateurs. . . . We became and are still professional amateurs. . . . If the gastronomic authorities and the cooking *caciques* were still in power, as in the Grévin Museum, more and more French, finally rid of the complexes of the Occupation, and then those of rediscovered wealth, became aware that eating well was not simply a guzzler's art, but one of the leisure-time activities of modern man.[43]

This whole speech rings true, but isn't it the same one Curnonsky made in evoking Escoffier, and Escoffier made in speaking of Carême, who said the same thing with regard to Massialot, etc.? It is the never-ending quarrel between the ancients and the moderns, expressing the ever-renewed vigor of a culture. Changes in tastes and habits are very heartening; what gets old, in the literature expressing such change, is the care taken in condemning predecessors. It is unjust, often petty, and absolutely useless, especially if one defends, as Gault and Millau do, the "true pleasure of the table, which is above all a choice, a selection." Would they dare claim that Monselet or Cur the prince felt no pleasure eating truffled pullets and puff pastries dripping with cream? These dishes ruined their health, of course, but with so much good cheer, as all accounts of their feasts make plain. And if the discourse was sometimes turgid, the epoch liked it that way. Furthermore, it was less so than the menus of certain pretentious and fashionable cooks, for whom the threat of ridicule does not interfere with their skill at creating an explosion of flavors.

We remain a bit perplexed at the ease with which cooks, professional critics, and amateur gastronomes have, for centuries, handled the anathema pronounced upon their predecessors or their contemporaries. What is conceivable for ideas seems a bit extreme for cooking, which merits a good dose of humor, since, except for Apicius and Vatel, no one generally kills himself over it! And especially since no cook requires anyone to consume what he prepares, unlike the architect, city planner, or politician. Like the painter, the musician, or the writer, he can only survive if he has customers, and the latter are generally willing. Nothing is more pleasing than a review, even when it is biting or biased, but nothing does it more harm than hiding behind dogmas that become outdated as quickly as fashions in clothing or music.

"*Nouvelle cuisine*," as the eating trend of the moment, for which Gault and Millau set the pace, was once more called, nevertheless closely corresponded to the entire post-1968 culture. That is what accounts for its success in all circles, in complete or partial form. Aside from a few inappropriate tirades, thanks to their familiar and often funny style, Gault and Millau attracted the *nouveaux riches* to restaurants headed by imaginative chefs, customers who, without these nods, would never have dared cross the Rubicon. After them, the whole press unleashed its fury.[44]

In 1973, they published the ten commandments of *nouvelle cuisine* in their magazine:

- You will not overcook things.
- You will use fresh, high-quality products.
- You will make your menu lighter.
- You will not be systematically modernistic.
- You will nevertheless look into what the new techniques have to offer you.
- You will avoid marinades, hanging game for too long, fermentation processes, etc.
- You will eliminate white and brown sauces.
- You will not ignore health.
- You will not rig your presentations.
- You will be inventive.[45]

There are some who claim that *nouvelle cuisine* never existed (those cooks who are anchored for good on *barbue Dugléré* and *blanquette de veau à l'ancienne*), others who say it is already very outmoded (those who met with a bit of success and are looking for a second wind without finding it), and still others, more clever, who pretend not to know what it is all about and declare with a simper that they only know of two kinds of cooking: good and bad (that is the position, more or less qualified, held by piano tenors).

In any case, the expression was immensely successful with the media, and cooks who drew their inspiration from it became as well known in time as some divas, a privilege that up until then only Raymond Oliver had enjoyed among the wider public, thanks to television. The reason was its appropriateness to the ambient culture: *nouvelle cuisine* shared in the rehabilitation of the body and the worship of nature, as well as that of truth and supremacy of the word.

The body: the great Escoffian and Curnonskian cuisine no longer corresponded to the principles of healthy eating and the canons of beauty, masculine or feminine. Social success had ceased to express itself in briochelike roundness, and Jane Birkin, with her image of the fashionable fourteenth-century lady in jeans, passed for the ideal of feminine beauty. Jean-Paul Aron has suggested a link—comical but incontestable—between this development in clothing fashion—in particular, the rehabilitation of briefs for men—and *nouvelle cuisine*:

> Under Louis-Philippe, an important man is also a man who weighs a lot. Then suddenly he wants to get undressed and as the women compete with him for the narrowest hips and flattest bellies, it is a matter, forthwith, of adapting nutrition to the dietetic norms of the aesthetic of the nude.[46]

That is the explanation for the success of "*grande cuisine minceur*," first conceived by Michel Guérard and then adopted by everyone. The quantities served were reduced, fats became rare, sauces gave way to "*jus très courts*," and vegetables came back into favor while starches fell into disgrace. But if Loiseau cooked with[47] water and Guérard with paraffin oil—at least in these diet recipes—all the great chefs continued to automatically set a mound or a plate of fine butter on each table and to finish their stocks and pan juices with butter in the great classical tradition, without considering all the butter that went into making appetizers and pastries, in addition to cream and whole milk. Fernand Point must be laughing in his grave, while customers continue to dig their own graves with their teeth!

Nature: the old principle of Brillat-Savarin and Curnonsky, according to which "good cooking is when things taste like what they are," is now more than ever at the fore, even if it is just as illusory today as in the past. Cooks swear to respect the freshness of the primary products, necessarily "in season" and "from the market."[48] Presentations are inspired by Japanese cooking, itself rooted in the Shintoist worship of nature. After Russian and then French service came Japanese service, which stripped the waiting staff of all initiative and gave the cook full responsibility for the appearance as well as the taste of the dish served. This kind of revolution was the fruit of the countless invitations to Japan from which many renowned French cooks had benefited for more than twenty years. It affected not only presentation but also cooking techniques. With his "Salmon Shizuo or The Return of Japan," Alain Senderens would even go so far as to finish soy sauce with butter, something many of his colleagues would also do henceforth with varying degrees of discretion.

The new serving style involved the use of large plates, hidden by silver dish covers between the kitchen and the table. When the chef put them down, he put his signature on the dish. This procedure has its devotees but also its bitter enemies, and the frequent diatribes by the *Monde* columnist, La Reynière, recall those of Antonin Carême against Russian service.[49] The difference is that water passes under the bridge more quickly today and that those who resist can easily be left behind by history, which explains the critics' necessary compromises. La Reynière himself does not fail to heap praises upon today's great chefs—Robuchon, Senderens, and many others—who nevertheless employ this technique.

Truth: there used to be a certain fondness for dishes served with a topping, stuffed, disguised, with a surprise center, prepared hot and served cold, baked in a crust, wrapped with fat, etc. This was the ancient tradition of the wild boar stuffed with suckling pigs, stuffed with capons, stuffed with partridge, stuffed with ortolans, or even with live birds flying out of the opening in the beast's stomach. Henceforth, down with the masks! Dishes were arranged on top of the sauce and not the other way around. The eye had to be able to distinguish everything entering into the plate's composition, and, when that was not entirely possible, the menu's flowing language had to fill in.

That is one of the guiding principles in contemporary culture. Such straight talk comes awfully close to exhibitionism, in its phobia of hypocrisy. In the exposed beams and bare stone of architectural restoration, the "high tech" style in decorating, tight jeans adopted as the universal article of clothing, rough language and feelings expressed without shame, we also see this post-1968 desire for absolute sincerity. Bernard Alexandre, a parish priest, shrewdly noted it with regard to his presbytery's restoration:

> The presbytery is a little sixteenth-century manor patched up and . . . disfigured in the nineteenth century by a bad roughcast. The opportunity came, thanks to that revolutionary month of May, to lay everything bare: the need for truth, authenticity. . . . To the devil with camouflage, hypocrisy! . . . I took part: hammering and smashing, with hard little blows, the thickly coated layers of accumulated paint.[50]

But this preoccupation shared by French cooks and their customers alike was not so easy to apply. No one was asking for Zen, and French cooking, like all of French culture, delights in cultivating the paradox of combining strict rigor with frivolity. As Claude Lévi-Strauss said, "A society's cuisine is a language in which it unconsciously expresses its structure, unless, without knowing better, it resigns itself to revealing its contradictions there."[51] Today's great cooking is a perfect illustration of that ambiguous game the French play with truth. What can we say about that great artisan, Joël Robuchon—without false modesty he refuses the title of artist—who rehabilitates such prosaic products as cod, potatoes, and cauliflower, but dresses the first in a subtle julienne of sautéed vegetables and a potent sauce, makes mashed potatoes into a veritable butter sauce, and hides under the puréed cauliflower a thick layer of caviar resting on lobster aspic? Breaking taboos is combined with a theatrical pursuit of surprises. The inventive expansion and constant renewal of present-day cuisine stands in stark contrast to the demise of family cooking, which, under the destructive influence of women joining the work force and the abolition of kitchen and dining rooms from modern apartments, has found itself reduced to a banal gustatory cliché.[52]

Love of the word, finally, is another key for understanding French *nouvelle cuisine*. Not content to become divas, cooks like to take the floor, something that few among them do as well as they cook, because they too willingly allow themselves to pontificate. Jean-Paul Aron has denounced this late twentieth century's logorrhea, which he considers to be its worst sin,[53] and which the voluble menus of fashionable restaurants well illustrate. According to him, the idea of the customer choosing from a pretentiously worded menu represents a grievous perversion, since the words are already almost enough to satisfy one's hunger and since the tongue is diverted from its gustatory function and set to wagging instead. This phenomenon is nothing new,[54] but it has become much more widespread since journalists have turned their attention to the lives, works, and vanities of the most popularized chefs.

The Expansion of Nouvelle Cuisine

A trend originating in Paris, *nouvelle cuisine* won over all of France in a few years—that is, with unheard-of speed for a cultural phenomenon. Of course, the accelerated way information now circulates provides the explanation for this. For a long time already, clothing fashion had been seized by the demon of rapid change, and we can find economic as well as cultural causes for such perpetual movement. Popular music, language, and literature are subject to the same sort of strictures. The stability of a style is vigorously condemned by pitiless censors who liken it to routine. Cycles in the progression of cooking used to be longer, and until the 1970s, the menus of prestigious restaurants evolved with a sensible slowness: one or two new dishes a year were added, at the very most. Thus, Lasserre's *canard à l'orange* remained the same in presentation and taste for nearly half a century, while the establishment's customers modified their clothing fashions every year. This was even more true in the provinces than in Paris: Fernand Point's *gratin de queues d'écrivisses* or Mère Brazier's *poularde demi-deuil* were veritable historical monuments.

Suddenly, the constant revision of menus became a measure of quality, and all the great establishments fell in step, almost to the point of absurdity. In the 1970s, tarragon was fashionable; thenceforth, it was the age of parsley. Sole became "old hat," making way for salmon, and today, faced with bland fish raised commercially in the fjords, it is time for cod, red mullet, indeed even sardines. Complex sauces were replaced by "*jus très courts*" and finished without butter (!). A whirlwind took shape in Paris. Raymond Oliver attests to that:

> When I arrived in Paris [the clientele] was set upon a very specific gastronomy that essentially boiled down to *langoustes mayonnaise* and *Chateaubriant béarnaise*, puffed potatoes. . . . Customers didn't want anything else, which, moreover, they wouldn't have known how to appreciate. For example, I remember having wood pigeon sent from

> my home and serving them rare, as was done in Langon; that is the way to bring out their flavor. The Parisian customers made me recook them.[55]

Oliver continues by disclosing one of the catalysts for *nouvelle cuisine*: travel, by customers but also by the cooks.

> In thirty-three years of cooking in Paris, I had periods, as a painter can have. . . . After my trip to Mexico, I had the tendency to make dishes very spicy, with a corn base, and then, after having gone to the South Sea Islands, I began serving fish raw or at least pink along the bone. . . . Tastes evolved to arrive, in the past few years, at that famouse *nouvelle cuisine* that has most of all revealed a desire to be creative. A very personal way of preparing dishes. That is what true cooking is, cooking that doesn't resemble the neighbor's.

Then comes the ultimate proof of a notable difference between Parisian *haute cuisine* and that of the provinces:

> I believe that the cooking done in Paris takes on exceptional qualities because it doesn't rely upon the easy recipes of the country you are passing through. In the provinces, you are hungry when you stop somewhere, and an appetizing suggestion is enough. . . . In Paris, it's completely different—I am speaking of high-quality restaurants here—the customer isn't hungry, he gets the food he needs at home. Therefore, at a restaurant, he must have a very varied, inventive menu.[56]

These lines, written only eight years ago, immediately became obsolete. Within a few years, creativity burst out all over France. As promoters and judges of *nouvelle cuisine*, Gault and Millau decided in 1977 to make a distinction in their guide between good restaurants serving traditional cuisines (black chef's hats) and those that had opted for "inventive" cuisines (red chef's hats); the second, of course, had preference. By the 1988 edition, things had progressed so quickly that there were more red chef's hats than black ones, and among the latter, you could count on the fingers of one hand those awarded three or four chef's hats. This is only one perspective, of course, but subjective as it is, it nevertheless reveals the velocity of the expansion of a cultural trait originating in Paris and spreading throughout French territory, including its least accessible corners (see maps 5 and 6).

Michel Guérard, a student of Jean Delaveyne in Bougival, was the forerunner. Overwhelmed with the success, beginning in 1965, of his obscure bistro in Asnières, he retired in 1972 to Eugénie-les-Bains, a no less obscure thermal spa in Landes. He contributed to its rejuvenation and success. From then on, the entire planet flocked to taste *la grande cuisine minceur* of the master or his *grande cuisine tout court*.[57] It is also at the end of the 1960s that we witness the renaissance of traditional provincial cooking.

The royal way, Paris–Lyons–the Mediterranean, was the first to be affected. Paul Bocuse at Collonges, Jean and Pierre Troisgros at Roanne, then Alain Chapel at Mionnay and Georges Blanc at Vonnas, Jacques Pic at Valence and a few others (Haeberlin at Illhaeusern, for example) modernized the register inherited from Fernand Point or Alexandre Dumaine. This was the period when that fraternity of successful chefs was established, allowing them to increase opportunities for becoming famous and prefiguring the *haute cuisine* employer's federation. Must they be reproached for this sense of stardom, as a certain number of disgruntled authors have done in the past few years?[58] Without placing them on a pedestal—which does no one any good—we are obliged to recognize that they all combined such prodigious creative effort with business sense, it is hard to know how to rebuke them while complimenting so many others. Their barely concealed pleasure at winning fame and wide public admiration is sometimes naive, but we must remember that generations of their predecessors never emerged from their unhealthy kitchens and that they all work inordinately hard, to the point of collapse, for some of them, in their prime: Jean Troisgros for example or, in 1990, Alain Chapel. It was the latter who wrote so lucidly that the secret is "a way of keeping in step with the fashion and of making it seem, by working hard, that one has taken the time to live."[59] If only that were so! The faults of great chefs have always been on par with their good qualities, and if we do not hesitate to criticize them, sometimes severely, they also deserve our affection, which alone allows for creativity, good work, and in the final analysis, the customer's satisfaction.

The success of a good chef—aided a bit by the guides and the media—no longer depends upon the place where they exercise their talents. Michel Bras enjoyed every honor and an international clientele . . . at Laguiole, in the heart of moonlike Aubrac. Going there is an adventure, in every sense of the word, as is going to Régis Marcon's at Saint-Bonnet-le-Froid, on the misty frontiers of Vivarais and Velay. Is there some snobbery on the part of the clients? Of course, but in the English sense of the term, that is to say, a solid sense of humor prompting them to follow impossible routes with the only expectation being an amazing meal!

In Paris, on the other hand, the desire for a change of scenery hardly affects lovers of fine cooking. Alain Dutournier has never succeeded in attracting to place Daumesnil the posh big-business clientele of the great hotels; hence, he prospers

GASTRONOMIC RESTAURANTS IN FRANCE ACCORDING TO THE 1988 *GAULT-MILLAU GUIDE*—TRADITIONAL CUISINE

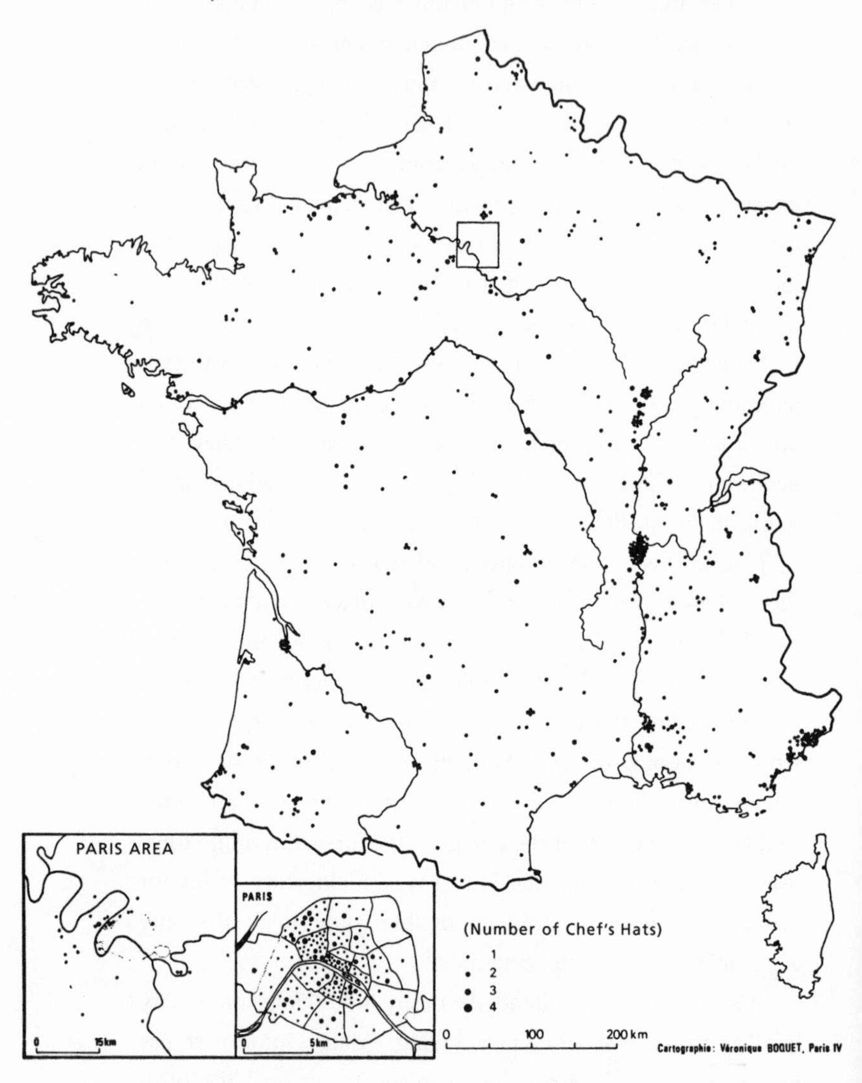

GASTRONOMIC RESTAURANTS IN FRANCE ACCORDING TO THE 1988 *GAULT-MILLAU GUIDE*—CREATIVE CUISINE

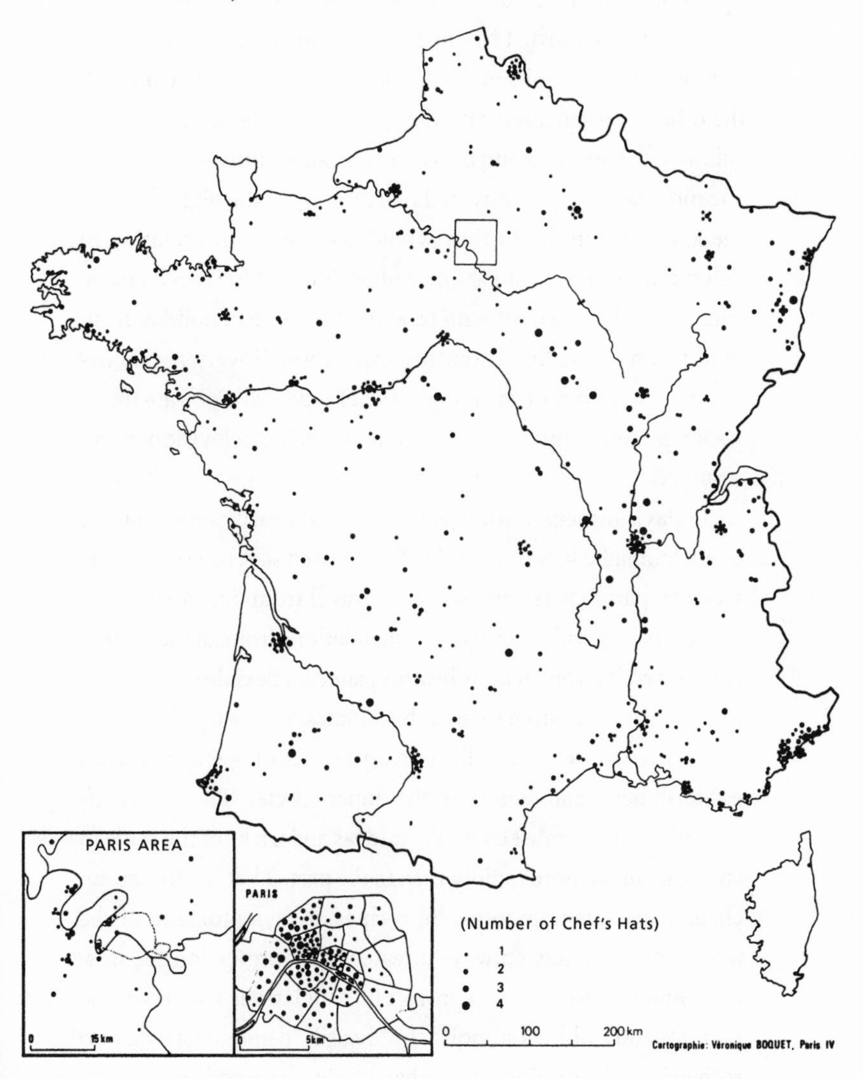

between the Ritz, Meurice, and Intercontinental, while Madame continues to satisfy the gourmands of eastern Paris. Of the great restaurants of Paris, the one farthest to the east (Ambroisie) opens onto the place des Vosges . . . which would be hard to compare to a suburb. The one farthest north, Edouard Carlier's Beauvilliers, has for its niche the side of the Montmartre hill. All the others are squeezed into the golden triangle or the western suburbs.[60] Nothing could be more natural: wealthy gourmets on vacation can take pleasure in daydreaming on the high plains of the Massif Central, but they would need much imagination to delight in slumming at Ivry or Aubervilliers. This is even more true for the less well off who treat themselves to a holiday from time to time and for whom the expression "lovely neighborhood" is not void of meaning. Michel Guérard's pot-au-feu at Asnières constituted an exception to which television is no stranger.

Today's principles for great cooking are easily disseminated by the nomadic habits of cooks. Chefs often see each other. The seconds, party chefs and assistants, travel from one great house to the next, provided with recommendations from all the former employers. Anyone who is healthy, appears flexible to his superiors and authoritative to his subordinates, who works hard and appreciates work done well has every chance of opening his own establishment and entering the inner circle. The "*tours de France*" made by most chefs allow ideas and tricks of the trade to circulate much more rapidly than in the past. That is why certain chefs' petty attempts to patent recipes are symptomatic of the megalomania that has always threatened the profession and now the commissions meant to protect it. Any lawyer who takes the time to study old cookbooks could easily demonstrate that no recipe is truly original. No, that is not the good fight to be fought; it is the one over the quality of raw materials.

EPILOGUE

Foods That Have a Soul: A Map of the Future for France

AT PRESENT FRENCH GOURMANDISM is experiencing paradoxical times. Never has there been so much talk about culinary creativity and cooks; never has so much literature—both scholarly and popular—been published on this theme. And yet, never has so little cooking been done at home. Each day, new fast food places open; just last year, the largest and the best pastry shop in central Dijon—a city that likes to think of itself as the gastronomy capital—gave way to a dispensary for sterile American food. Will French food lose its charm and its soul? Will discourse become a substitute for reality, that is, a means for creating the desire for pleasure (without ever attaining it) and not for preparing food, and especially not for extending and embellishing upon it? Will Brillat-Savarin's legacy end in farce? The question is worth asking, because it involves a major aspect of our lifestyle, our culture, and our economy, developing over the many centuries we have just passed through.

France, What Have You Made of Your Gourmandism?

"I estimate that eight or nine out of ten customers know nothing about the culinary arts," exclaims the *maître d'*, Antoine Ventura, spokesperson for a usually discreet profession, but in a prime position to judge the eating expertise of the French.[1] A bitter reflection from a man disappointed in his contemporaries, to whom he has devoted all his talent and from whom he would like more appreciation of the efforts made in real restaurants! And alas, he is not alone in his point of view. It was already the opinion of the much missed critic, Henri Viard, who was so deeply troubled by the development of fast food. Joël Robuchon, one of the most subtle and modest contemporary cooks, complains:

> Only a small number of French possess refined palates. The French believe they have innate knowledge in the gastronomic domain as in the domain of wines. Whereas nothing is further from the truth. France is one of the world's leading wine-producing countries, and its inhabitants don't know wines! On the other hand, I am astonished to note the level of knowledge among certain foreigners. The Swiss, for example, are great connoisseurs. And the Japanese show real curiosity: they are very attentive in trying to understand and to taste what they are served. That is what refinement is.[2]

In response to a question about his own customers—whom we might believe to be more enlightened or whom he might want to spare out of concern for his business—Robuchon does not hesitate to speak frankly:

> This might surprise you, but the number of those who possess real knowledge and have refined palates is extremely limited there as well. And it has nothing to do to with social class. Indeed, people from all stations come to my place, and the least wealthy are far from being the least knowledgeable. . . . If 20 or even 10 percent of the customers in my dining room had truly refined taste, I would be happy.

We hear the same lament from Michel Guérard:

> The French imagine themselves to have amazing palates, whereas they can very often be found lacking. It is terrible to think that there are not even ten cooks out of a hundred who know how to taste wine, while they all believe themselves to be great experts. . . . If we tried to determine what proportion of the French population were connoisseurs, I would say less than 15 percent. The rest eat, but do not know how to tell if a mackerel is cooked well or badly. But we also have to talk about the cooks: many of them are not gourmets and thus are wasting their time in this profession.[3]

The results of an IPSOS poll done in 1989 by the *Gault-Millau* magazine confirm these opinions.[4] One percent of those polled were able to give all the right answers to a dozen simple questions, 37 percent to five or more questions; 12 percent knew that the four basic tastes were salty, sweet, bitter, and sour; 42 percent could name three varieties of potatoes; 5 percent knew that there was no cream in a Béarnaise sauce; 28 percent knew that a capon was a castrated and fattened rooster. More astonishing still: 47 percent did not know the type of milk used for making Roquefort, 90 percent did not know what noble rot is, and 97 percent did not know that the grape used in Beaujolais is the Gamay! The objection could be raised that what was tested here is intellectual knowledge and that the results have nothing to do with gustatory refinement. All the same, the French exhibit a striking indifference to the nature of what they eat, even as labels provide more and more information and the press accords much more importance to these questions than it did in the past.

According to a certain number of authors, those minor prophets of doom, it will be very difficult to regain lost ground, and good French cooking is going out with a bang, applauded by those in charge of the farm-produce industry. That is the pessimistic thesis defended by Jean-Claude Marcel in a recent vitriolic and nearly convincing tract.[5] For him, the fluorescent, vacuum-packed meats and vegetables, the omelet in a packet and the spray-can chocolate mousse are coming very close to replacing all fresh products on the market. Agribusiness has gained control of the entire food chain, from agriculture to distribution, and including agronomical research, the press, and health food. The most reputable chefs themselves are all more or less linked by contract to large conglomerates that use them, perhaps as advisors but especially as alibis: Guérard with Findus, Robuchon with Fleury-Michon, Dutournier with Monoprix, Michel Oliver with Casino, etc., none of them, moreover, serving in their establishments the pastry shells they put their signatures on. . . . Here is an example, among many others, of Marcel's terrible anger:

> This blind, frenzied, systematic industrialization, which has been the policy of those in power, no matter what side they are on, for thirty years, savagely destroys our heritage and our ecological stability, threatens our health, condemns millions of people to unemployment and poverty, pollutes our bodies and our minds. I am not exaggerating.[6]

Is this anger put on? Is this hotel and restaurant school professor only expressing his jealousy of the great and much admired chefs and gazing back nostalgically on the good old times? If the power of the farm-produce industry is a new phenomenon, regret over the foods of the past is not. There are always those cooks, writers, and gourmands who think we ate much better in the past. "A good dinner is a rare thing today. Gastronomy is like poetry: it is in total decline," one wrote, for example, in the *Courrier de Paris* on March 27, 1858.[7] Without avoiding the real questions posed by Jean-Claude Marcel, we must note nevertheless that food and drink have not always beckoned happily from their plates and glasses.

We must not forget that, until very recently, even if women spent a certain amount of time cooking, most French people ate a barely sufficient and unvaried diet: little or no meat; cabbage soup; potatoes; stale bread; water, often of questionable quality, mixed to varying degrees with mediocre wine; few foods with vitamins for six months out of the year. Natural food, certainly, but only healthy up to a certain point. To keep salted or smoked pork is not an easy operation in all seasons, as is true for potatoes that sprout and grains and vegetable that mold so easily. People undoubtedly ate a little better in the cities, but workers had to be content with the contents of a mess kit, reheated if possible and eaten on the run. As for the school or company cafeterias, you would have to be awfully hungry to eat in them. Without wishing in any way to excuse current practices, we might recall that in the 1960s, a good number of chickens tasted like the fishmeal they were fed; veal calves were almost systematically given hormones; if saltwater fish were fresh at all, it was only in Paris; milk products were unreliable; and you had to go a long way to find acceptable ice cream. The first processed foods were insipid to extremes, indeed even chemical in taste (desserts, corned beef, margarine, tomato sauce, bouillon cubes, etc.). And remember what served as wine for the vast majority of French people? Aramon from Languedoc fortified with 14 percent wine from Algeria! In restaurants, kitchen conditions were often repugnant; cooks ruined their own health there, as did their regular customers who filled up on overcooked dishes (thus avoiding food poisoning), drowned in Espagnole sauce finished with butter.

On the other hand, a certain number of mothers knew how to prepare vegetable soup, pâtés, *pot-au-feu*, daube, *blanquette* and Burgundy stews, tarts, and various specialties varying from region to region. Not all of them, far from it! How many of them, poor and entirely ignorant of the art of eating well on little money, served noodles one meal out of two and potatoes the rest of the time, boiled in water or fried in bad grease? Jean-Claude Marcel is wrong to silently pass over these realities, of which he must be aware. It weakens his argument and leads food manufacturers and cooks, whom he justly denounces, to shrug their shoulders rather than to consider what he says.

The French agribusiness industry is, like all economic activities, concerned with realizing the highest possible profits. It has known how to respond perfectly to the French desire to consume more meat, milk products, a variety of vegetables and greens, sugar, delicatessen products, and precooked dishes. It has achieved this—why deny it?—by increasing agricultural productivity, that is, by encouraging farmers to be productive, with the blessing of successive agriculture ministers, the Brussels Commission, farm unions, and the entire rural community who believed progress was finally coming to call. The fact that this process sacrificed a measure of quality, namely, the richness of the products' taste, was simply overlooked. That is why sounding the alarms, including Jean-Claude Marcel's, for all its bias, is useful. Nothing is ever fatal, irreparable. The French have the food they find acceptable, or if we want to be harsh, the food they deserve. The same goes for their landscapes, their housing, their politicians, their artists, etc.

And so, the situation is serious: few French still know how to choose or taste their food; certain cooks and many agribusiness and food distribution firms take advantage of their ignorance, and sometimes of their snobbery. So be it! But it would not take very much to reverse the engines: the will of a few politicians and agricultural and agribusiness leaders, and a well-orchestrated public opinion campaign, as people know how to organize these days for much less worthy causes. Perhaps the circumstances have never been so favorable: the country's economic prosperity, the end of totalitarian ideologies, an emerging thirst for inner cultivation parallel to that for material consumption. The advantages that French society could gain from a revival of gourmandism are much less trivial than we might be tempted to believe.

A Plea for Taste

The French would benefit from recalling that they have never scorned taste over the course of their history, thus bringing back into cultivation this sense that has partially gone to seed. It cannot be said too often that to master the taste buds, that is, to be able to discern what you are eating or drinking, develops the intelligence just as much as the practice of music or painting, and provides, as all the arts do, immense and noble satisfactions. Defending this point of view prompts smiles in many circles considering themselves cultivated or intellectual, or still attached to a disembodied spirituality.

The child psychologist, Matty Chiva, has made herself this

idea's theorist, and the oenologist, Jacques Puisais, its practitioner. Both of them know how to make the idea obvious enough to anyone who takes the trouble to read them. "For reasons based in the very structure of the sensory apparatus and the nervous system," writes Matty Chiva, "taste, like smell, has a profound and immediate emotional resonance."[8] For Jacques Puisais and Catherine Pierre,

> a child who is only fed on rice and chocolate milk, for example, seems to us to enjoy too limited a sensorial spectrum to blossom harmoniously. Doesn't he deny himself all the rest, often in reaction against adults, sometimes too authoritative, sometimes too lax? A deprivation all the more regrettable because each sense organ is absolutely unique. Thousands of cells come into play in the gustatory Stradivarius, which we must use with intelligence, instead of brutalizing this fine instrument in barbaric youth.[9]

An anecdote Jacques Puisais relates highlights remarkably well the contribution of what could be called a dietetic of sensibility and of culture:

> I was with professor Matty Chiva. . . . A young woman was interviewing us and asked the following question: "My children, seven and nine years old, never want to eat and I am looking for a medication to remedy this situation." . . . I asked her, "Do you like to cook?" The response was clear: "No." I explained to her, "How could you expect your children to want to sit down at the table when, from their earliest childhood, the fact of seeing you grab the handle of the frying pan conveyed to them,

> through your movements and gestures, a kind of torture; your children don't want their mother's face to appear so joyless." The mother was a little shaken and said to us, "But then, it's my fault!" And my response was clear: "Yes."[10]

Following other paths, biologists arrive at these same conclusions, in particular Jean-Marie Bourre,[11] who advocates a diet agreeable to the brain and thus to intelligence: "Only carefully chosen foods allow the brain to develop, maintain itself, and function. Only a proper diet authorizes the organism to perform its duties." His analysis of the long-term effects of consuming fast foods and drinks can make you shudder.

We still do not have precise knowledge regarding the operations of the complex chain linking food to thought. That is the subject of current neurobiological research. What is certain at present is that the brain cannot maintain proper coordination of the body and the thought processes without a satisfactory diet. We also know that its needs are very diverse and that it is dangerous to limit too severely the consumption of lipids, sugars, salt, not to mention countless proteins, vitamins, trace elements, etc. Man and his brain are what they eat; this is not only a saying ("tell me what you eat . . ."), it is a biological reality. We know, through experiments using animals, that the neurons and neurotransmitters can suffer from certain deficiencies. Moreover, and Jean-Marie Bourre energetically defends this point of view, eating must give pleasure and not be limited to a mechanical ingestion of calories. He advocates a true cerebral diet/ethic combining biochemical equilibrium and the pursuit of *joie de vivre*.

This point of view is all the more credible in that it does not result in an all-purpose formula, and especially not some kind of dietetic moralizing. "The day when science organizes all our meals," contemplates Jean-Marie Bourre, "the world will stop turning, because it will have lost the desire to live. Above all, let us not forget that the brain is also the organ that allows for the aesthetic pleasure of gastronomy."

To the man on the street, it may seem pedantic to present scholarly theories on the relationship between the dawning of intelligence and the rewards of eating well. Nevertheless, it is the only discourse that can curb the current rejection of traditions. We must make mothers, who read magazines and special reports in order to turn their children into future Nobel prize winners, aware of what teachers on all levels, psychologists, pediatricians, and professional educators say. We must convince them of the mindlessness and degeneracy that no doubt will surface in their dear little ones, and to an even greater extent in their descendants, if they continue to neglect their gustatory education. It is important for them to understand that making children eat everything, from the time they are *in utero* and nursing, is an essential means of letting them blossom. Why must mothers, for example, deprive themselves of garlic and asparagus during this important phase of the child's sensorial apprenticeship? To assign baby foods and cereal a complementary or supplementary role is not an insult to the progress and the liberation of women; very much the opposite. We grant so much importance today to the awakening of intelligence in infants that we must make this very sensitive chord resonate in those who are responsible for them.

What families can and must rediscover, schools can, too, without major difficulty. That is what Alfred Mame and Jacques Puisais try to demonstrate within the framework of the French Institute of Taste, which has its headquarters in Tours.[12] One of the principal activities of this association is organizing educational sessions on sensory awakening aimed at schoolchildren from eight to twelve years old, to the great satisfaction of both the students and their teachers. In collaboration with them, the Paris Education Offices have recently attempted a very successful operation. Why not organize a national campaign?

What is true for children is even more true for adults. It is never too late to learn that the three daily meals need not be annoying drudgery, but can be high points in daily life, providing both pleasure and an understanding of the world. Taste and smell, which is so close to it, are as perfectible as the musical sense or the art of painting, and this is true regardless of age. Consider the virtuosity of Dom Pérignon's palate at the end of his life:

> This unique man retained into decrepit old age a delicacy of taste so singular that by tasting a grape, he could correctly discern the canton that had produced it. He was presented with a basket of grapes collected from local vineyards and from the Cumières region; he tasted them, arranging each according to the soil it came from, and noting with assurance the places suitable for the best-quality wine, relative to the heat or humidity of summer and fall.[13]

Collecting sensations on one's plate and in one's glass and transforming them into emotions: this is to give life its contours, to move from material contingencies toward a communion with the world. But to achieve this, you have to make the effort (as this is not a reflex) to vary your diet according to the circumstances, your health, your mood, the people with whom you are eating, the place you happen to find yourself, the season, the weather, etc. Once again, financial means have no bearing on this philosophy, because nutritive shams often cost more that those foods having the "right taste"—to adopt Jacques Puisais's expression—which can be as humble as a soft-boiled egg and buttered strips of bread. It is important not to be slave to any one consistency (tenderness, for example[14]) or any one taste (sweetness). The crispy, the sticky, or the bitter can provide intense sensations, once the palate gets used to them.

Describing his childhood vacations in Maurienne, Alain Chapel so marvelously expresses what for him was cooking with feeling, as opposed to the melodrama performed by a certain number of chefs, inflated with expertise and artistic pretensions but unaware of their surroundings:

> Rye bread, broad bean soup, sautéed apples (delicious dumplings), butter and cheeses from the high mountain pastures, they all testified to an impoverished cuisine, resolutely lacking in all disguise, all artifice, all magic. Something resolutely material that still strikes me today as a reality a bit eroded, a bit erased in the heads of certain chefs. At Albiez, in any case, at a table without crystal or table manners, I learned that cooking is much more than recipes. It is the products, first and above all, and the feelings that are no doubt rooted in the landscape, the faces, a familiar everyday life, a happiness more ample than the table. The sincerity of beings falling somewhere on this side of economic constraints and the game of appearances. The sincerity of beings like that of things, of broad beans or of rye.[15]

And Chapel continues in an oratorical flight constituting a marvelous homage to true geography:

> It was the good fortune of cooks like Paul Bocuse to have had a rural education. The foundation for their creations

lies there, something that forever distances them from a sophistication lost in the clouds. We well know that certain cooks today consider themselves inventors and would like to present their truffle sorbet or their puff pastry sole with Chantilly cream at some Lépine cooking competition. They make themselves happy, they believe, in hatching some novel thing, not grown under natural sunlight but in the neon of their hodgepodge ideas. In consideration of which they concoct for us dishes as useless and complicated as translations of mediocre detective novels into alexandrines. These practices are very different from those that rule in the country, requiring a precise knowledge of one's place. Rather than privilege originality at any cost, the cook must attempt to capture what remains of a heritage, to continually question himself about culinary idiosyncrasies, to try to know the deep motivations behind them.

The Geography of Eating Well, Eating Well as a Geographer

The French have very fixed ideas about the geography of eating well in their country. At least that is the impression emerging from the IFOP poll done thirty years ago, which would no doubt produce the same results if it were repeated today (see map 7).[16] Among the regions proposed to those polled, Perigord won a majority of the votes. With regard to starred restaurants, this opinion is perfectly unjustified. However, it is true that throughout the southwest, a certain number of modest establishments still exist where you can eat heartily at little cost. Moreover—and this is probably the key to understanding the results—Perigord is one of the oldest regions producing foie gras and truffles, mythic foods that most French people, like for-

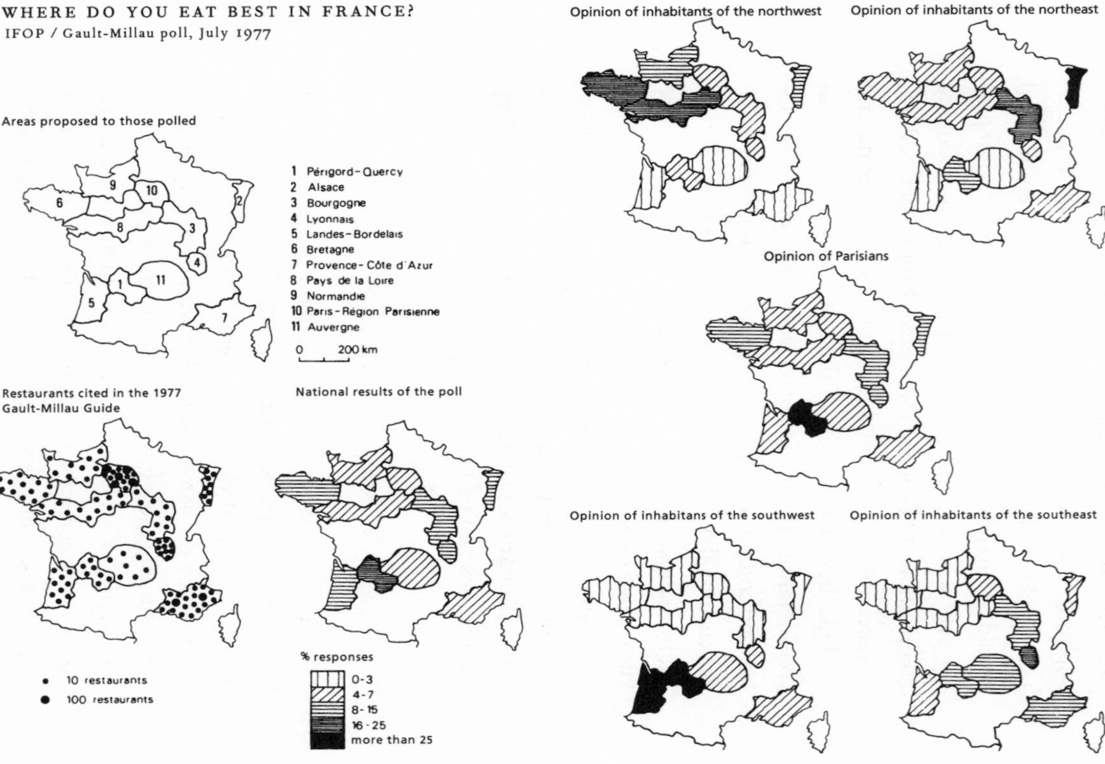
WHERE DO YOU EAT BEST IN FRANCE?
IFOP / Gault-Millau poll, July 1977
Areas proposed to those polled
1 Périgord-Quercy
2 Alsace
3 Bourgogne
4 Lyonnais
5 Landes-Bordelais
6 Bretagne
7 Provence-Côte d'Azur
8 Pays de la Loire
9 Normandie
10 Paris-Région Parisienne
11 Auvergne
0 200 km
Restaurants cited in the 1977 Gault-Millau Guide
10 restaurants
100 restaurants
National results of the poll
% responses
0-3
4-7
8-15
16-25
more than 25
Opinion of inhabitants of the northwest
Opinion of inhabitants of the northeast
Opinion of Parisians
Opinion of inhabitans of the southwest
Opinion of inhabitants of the southeast

eigners, dream about. The mediocre opinion the French hold, no matter where they are from, with regard to Paris and Provence–Côte d'Azur may be explained by the restaurant prices in those two areas, but not at all by the number of good eating places or, especially in the case of Paris, by the abundance and quality of the exceptional food products found there. An analysis of the results according to the region of origin of those polled reveals a chauvinism we may find surprising among people who consider themselves objective connoisseurs, but that is one of their major characteristics. Each French person constructs for himself a gastronomic geography centered upon his own place of origin or reference, which recalls the humor of Glyn Daniel, the famous English prehistorian, who thought one could only eat well along the routes allowing him to reach Carnac from Le Havre and Lascaux from Calais (see map 8)![17]

Rootedness is one of the great subjects for nostalgia among the French; the little homeland is a "place of memory." This is Ariadne's thread, which must be followed to give the French back "the right taste." Opposing mass marketing and the food-produce industry is a delaying action that has no chance of success and, despite the adventure it offers, profits no one. It would result in food shortages, as well as an agricultural slump and unemployment in the prosperous food services and the industrial branch.

On the other hand, it is necessary to work for overall improvement in food quality, by stopping the homogenization now underway and developing a respect for regional diversity. Contrary to the received ideas of a certain economic system, this process is perfectly compatible with the modernization of agriculture and agribusiness, as it is with mass marketing.

Until now, wine growing has provided the best examples here. There are quite a few reasons for nervousness in Cham-

GASTRONOMIC FRANCE ACCORDING TO GLYN DANIEL, ENGLISH PREHISTORIAN

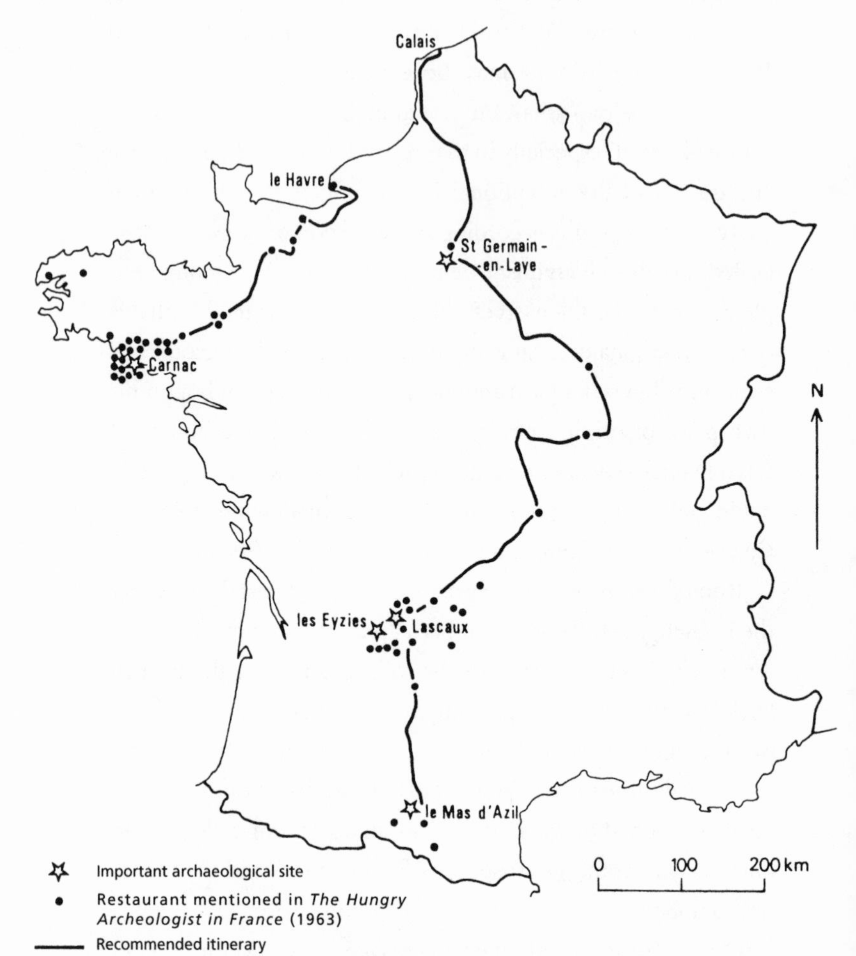

pagne or Beaujolais. We may regret the increasing popularity of certain easy-to-grow and only mildly interesting types of vines, like the Gamay, as well as the abusive price increases in Sancerre or Burgundy, especially in Chablis or between Dijon and Santenay. But thirty years ago, the south produced only vile potions. The local wines had not been restored since the phylloxera epidemic. Bordelais was entangled in its scandals and its illicit blending. A good number of small wine growers from all areas had hardly mastered fermentation, let alone cultivating wines. The rigorous and intelligent policies of the INAO allowed for the rapid decline of mass wine growing and the expansion of all quality wine growing based on local vine stocks, proven viticultural methods like vinification, and limited yield. The vast increase in local labels, sometimes by village or even by region, crowned the efforts of the entire profession: wine growers, cooperatives, merchants, oenologists, restaurant owners.

Among many examples, we could cite Cahors, Costières de Nîmes, Haut-Poitou wines, and the Hautes-Côtes of Nuits and of Beaune. We could salute the extraordinary improvement in quality among the generic Bordeaux, the Premières-Côtes and the middle-class *crus*, the Côtes-du-Rhônes, and the wines of Loire. One of the most spectacular recoveries was that of the Alsace wines. This region produced hardly any good wines following World War II. Today it has managed to put together a family of good, or even great, wines, ranging from typed, often well-vinified, and low-priced vintages to the regional *grand cru* and rarities from late harvests and selections of noble grapes. The effort has come as much from the cooperatives, like the Eguisheim cooperative, as from certain enlightened wine growers/merchants, like Hugel in Riquewihr, and restaurant owners, like the Haeberlin brothers in Illhaeusern. These latter are not the only ones in France working for the renaissance of forgotten or overlooked vineyards: Marc Meneau has begun the replanting of Vézely, Georges Blanc is attempting to boost the prestige of Mâcon, and Michel Guérard, that of Jurançon.

The French taste for wine is at the height of development. There are greater and greater numbers of French people who appreciate *appellation contrôlée* wines, in which they are increasingly able to recognize originality and, with the help of travel, regional expression. Here is a phenomenon—and one, we hope, that is more than a fleeting fashion—comparable to the current infatuation with opera. It is up to the wine-related profession to transform these signs of interest into habits, but it is also up to consumers to require ever more from producers and distributors in terms of quality and sincerity, that is, being sensitive and aware in their methods for cultivating and producing wine. What profound pleasure there is in rediscovering in the taste of wine a landscape, an atmosphere, a wine grower's personality, and, it goes without saying, the characteristics of a vintage!

Thus, high technology and industrialization have not destroyed French wine. In the superstores, we find excellent wines (and mediocre ones, too, of course!) at very attractive prices. Moreover, in this area, mass marketing has not killed off the little guys, and many wine growers live quite well by selling exclusively to private individuals with whom they maintain cooperative arrangements.

Why couldn't this success with wine be transposed to all agribusiness products? Some evidence of consumer interest would be enough for BSN, SOPAD-Nestlé, Bel, Olida, and so many other companies to organize themselves accordingly. Nothing stands in the way of controlling a vast distribution network and of collecting distinctive and tasty produce, fruits of a region and a culture. Antoine Riboud, the chairman and chief executive officer of BSN, a passionate admirer of Rostropovitch, cannot remain insensitive to such ideas. He could probably be fairly easily convinced of the necessity of such a revolution if he had proof that his contemporaries could prosper by it . . . and that his own enterprise could make as much money. Hasn't Edouard Leclerc been a bit of a convert by distributing many local products from small companies in his supermarkets?

INRA (*Institut national de la recherche agronomique*), an organization that, for a long time, spearheaded productivity, technocracy, and standardization, seems to have glimpsed the limits of its actions. It recently decided to collaborate with the *haute cuisine* employers' federation in an effort to promote high-quality vegetable species and animal breeds. Day-long conferences were organized around apples and beef cattle. With regard to the latter, for example, important guest chefs in a blindfolded taste test overwhelmingly selected the grilled meat from a Limousin cow put out to pasture, a true "outsider," rating it far above the usual favorite, a classic Charolais beef. To understanding this apparently surprising result, we must be aware that Charolais cattle breeders have never managed to agree on breeding techniques guaranteeing the consumer quality meat, and they are still too susceptible to the productivity sirens' song.[18]

Once more, quality, that is, the production of foods that speak to the body and the imagination, is profitable. Even better, it is the only possible map of the future for French agriculture, sensitive as it is to the least fluctuations in international exchange rates, so hard to control in these times of overproduction in rich countries. Reversing the engines is risky, but there are enough examples of success to make all French farmers think at times of the chances they let slip by. We could applaud, for example, the Isigny cooperative, from which we get such marvelous Camembert, butter, and cream; or the

Echiré cooperative, whose butter the Elysée, the Monaco palace, and the best restaurants in France fight over;[19] or Lionel Poilâne, who manages to provide good bread to all Parisians, New Yorkers, and a few other world citizens who make the effort to find one of his retail outlets.

The day will come when Marseilles bread will not taste the same as Chartres bread, Rouen steak will not taste like Nancy steak, and Guérande salt will not taste like Aigues-Mortes salt. Utopia, the pious hope of the overfed highbrow? Maybe not.

Suddenly aware of the failure of interventionism dominated by large-scale economic research, the encouragement of productivity, and thus the dramatic indebtedness of farmers, the Ministry of Agriculture has finally come to understand that it is important to grant priority to foods with a clear personal touch. Henceforth, all products can, like wine, benefit from an *appellation d'origine contrôlée*. It is significant that, not counting Communist Party members, this bill was passed unanimously by the deputies of the French National Assembly.[20] In November 1989, Henri Nallet, who was then Minister of Agriculture, gathered his European Common Market allies at Beaune to convince them that this policy was well founded.[21] He deserves thanks—because this was a great first step—but we have a long way to go before we convince our northern neighbors or even our own farmers.

But all is not lost! Let the French convince themselves to eat well once again and they will remedy the disease of languor that sometimes affects them. They will salvage their optimism, and for certain, a great chunk of their economy, in a Europe and a developed world that has too willingly thrown their gourmandism out the window. A supplement to well-being is priceless; no one can lose by treating oneself to it.

NOTES

Introduction: On France's Gastronomic Passion

1. "Impérialisme culinaire?" *Le Magazine*, Alianza francesa de Mexico, 42 (February 1990): 16 (I owe this reference to Bernard Lacombe). Again in this astonishing text we read: "The French are just naturally inclined to transform anything that moves or grows on their soil into delectable dishes."
2. *Le Nouveau Guide Gault-Millau* April 1977:42.
3. Philéas Gilbert, *L'Art culinaire* (Paris, 1884), II:81–82. Also see Jean-Paul Aron, *Le Mangeur du XIXe siècle* (Lausanne: Ex Libris, 1974), 184.
4. Taken up again since by a private group.
5. Jean Ferniot, *Rapport aux ministres sur la promotion des arts culinaires* (Paris: Ministères de la Culture et de l'Agriculture, April 1985).
6. Which does not negate the fact that Alsatian food and wines played no small role in the choice of Bergheim-Ribeauville as the site for Sony's very large industrial complex. *Le Monde*, September 1, 1988.
7. Lu Wenfu, *Vie et passion d'un gastronome chinois* (Arles: Ed. Philippe Pécquier–UNESCO, 1988).
8. Foretaste by Françoise Sabban in ibid., 14–15 and 18–19.

9. J.-C. Nemeitz, *Séjour à Paris, instruction fidèle pour les voyageurs de condition* (Leyde, 1727). Quoted by Philippe Gillet, *Par mets et par vins. Voyages et gastronomie en Europe (XVIIe–XVIIIe siècles)* (Paris: Payot, 1985), 59–60.
10. Philippe Mordacq, *Le Menu. Histoire illustrée* (Paris: Robert Laffont, 1989).
11. *Le Figaro*, March 18, 1981.
12. Karen Blixen, *Le Dîner de Babette* (Paris: Gallimard, 1988), 27–75.
13. József Venesz, *Les Plaisirs de la table* (Budapest: Corvina, 1958), 5.
14. *Le Figaro*, August 17, 1987.
15. The role English wine consumption plays in the market has been well described by Henri Enjalbert, *Histoire de la vigne et du vin. L'avènement de la qualité* (Paris: Bordas, 1975); see 96–103 and 116–117.
16. La Reynière, "Fernand Point, le pyramidal," *Cuisine* et *Vins de France* 374 (March 1982): 33–35.
17. Alphonse Daudet, *Lettres de mon moulin* (Paris: Grands Ecrivains, 1984), 146.
18. Joseph Berchoux, *La Gastronomie ou l'homme des champs à table. Poème didactique en IV chants pour servir de suite à l'Homme des Champs* (1801; reprint, Grenoble: Glénat, 1989).
19. O. Bloch and W. von Wartburg, *Dictionnaire étymologique de la langue française* (Paris: PUF, 1975).
20. Françoise Charpentier, "Le symbolisme de la nourriture dans le *Pantagruel*," in J.-C. Margolin and R. Sauzet, eds., *Practiques et discours alimentaires à la Renaissance* (Paris: Maisonneuve et Larose, 1982), 219–231; see 228.
21. "Nourritures," special issue 2a of *Livraisons* (1981), 24.
22. Alexandre Dumas, *Le Grand Dictionnaire de cuisine* (Paris: Henri Veyrier, 1974).
23. Michel Guérard, *La Grande Cuisine minceur* (Paris: Robert Laffont, 1976). Jean-Louis Flandrin develops this idea in "Médicine et habitudes alimentaires anciennes," in Margolin and Sauzet, *Practiques et discours alimentaires à la Renaissance*, 85–95.
24. Salvador Dali, *Dîners de Gala* (Paris: Draeger, 1967), 4.
25. Alain Chapel, *La cuisine, c'est beaucoup plus que des recettes!* (Paris: Le Livre de Poche, 1987), 65.
26. Michel Onfray, *Le Ventre des philosophes* (Paris: Grasset, 1989), 21.

1. France: The Land of Milk and Honey or the Old Country of Gourmands?

1. Roland Gadille, *Le Vignoble de la Côte bourguignonne. Fondements physiques et humains d'une viticulture de haute qualité* (Paris: Les Belles Lettres, 1967), 304.
2. René Pijassou, *Un grand vignoble de qualité: Le Médoc* (Paris: Tallandier, 1980), 559–560. In addition to oral information provided by René Pijassou.
3. Roger Dion, "Querelle des Anciens et des Modernes sur les facteurs de la qualité du vin," *Annales de géographie* 1952:431; republished in *Le Paysage et la vigne. Essais de géographie historique* (Paris: Payot, 1990).
4. Ibid.
5. Alphonse Daudet, *Lettres de mon moulin* (Paris: Grands Ecrivains, 1984), 53.
6. Jean-Robert Pitte, preface, in Roger Dion, *Le Paysage et la vigne*, 7–20; and "Le mariage d'amour de la France et du vin," *L'Histoire* 136 (September 1990): 88–90.
7. Auguste Escoffier, *Souvenirs inédits* (Marseilles: Jeanne Laffitte, 1985), 191.
8. The same is true for landscapes. Those in France are not, in any way, more varied than elsewhere. See Jean-Robert Pitte, *Histoire du paysage français* (Paris: Tallandier, 1986), I:241.
9. Paul de Courselles and Sixte Delorme, *En route avec l'oncle Mistral* (Paris: Librairie Ducrocq, 1900), 5. I owe this reference to Xavier de Planhol.
10. Elizabeth David, *French Provincial Cookery* (London: Penguin, 1978), 17.
11. Interview with Jean-Robert Pitte, *Gault-Millau* (October 1989):45.
12. Athenaeus, IV:36 (C 151–152), adapted from Poseidonios. Also see Paul-Marie Duval, *Pourquoi "Nos ancêtres les Gaulois"* (Paris: PUF, 1982), 20–27.
13. Ibid.
14. Diodorus, V:25–27.
15. In particular, among the Greeks. See Henri Enjalbert, *Histoire de la vigne et du vin. L'avènement de la qualité* (Paris: Bordas, 1976), 25.
16. Roger Dion, *Histoire de la vigne et du vin en France des origines au XIX*[e] *siècle* (Paris: Self-published, 1959).

17. Strabo, IV:4.3 (C. 199).
18. Strabo, IV:4.3 (C. 197).
19. Varro, *Rerum Rusticarum. De Agriculture*, II:4. Also see Patrice Meniel, *Chasse et élavage chez les Gaulois* (Paris: Les Hespérides, 1987). Jérôme Carcopino was a bit optimistic in thinking it was possible to map the oak forests in Gaul beginning from the references to hams. See M. Devèze's remark following Monique Clavel: "La forêt en Gaule d'après les sources littéraires," *Actes du colloque sur la forêt. Annales littéraires de l'université de Besançon* 88 (1967): 43.
20. Pliny, 10, 53.
21. Numerous references given by Jacques André, *L'Alimentation et la cuisine à Rome* (Paris: Les Belles Lettres, 1981), 154. Also see Agnès Benoît, "Le repas dans la Gaule celtique et le repas dans la Gaule romaine," *Les Français à table* (Paris: Musée national des arts et des traditions populaires, 1985), 64–69 and 72–81.
22. Ausone, *Epist.*, 7, V:1–2 and 9, V:18–19 and 25–40. Quoted in André, *L'Alimentation et la cuisine à Rome*, 106.
23. Bertrand Hell, "Manières de boire, manières de vivre; les buveurs de bière en Alsace," in *Nourritures, sociétés et religions. Commensalités, Eurasie* 1 (1900): 26–37.
24. Jean-Robert Pitte, "Le vin des brumes. Le renaissance de la viticulture dans les îles Britanniques," *Campagnes et littoraux d'Europe. Mélanges offerts à Pierre Flatrès*, special issue of *Hommes et terres du Nord* 1988:266–272. Also in Alain Huetz de Lemps, et al., *Le vins de l'impossible* (Grenoble: Glénat, 1990), 31–35.
25. Proprietor of the restaurant Le Crocodile, Strasbourg, interview by author, October 1989.
26. Morris E. Chafetz, *Du bon usage de l'alcool* (Paris: Robert Laffont, 1966), 83.
27. "Wine is inseparable from great cooking," says Antoine Ventura, one of the great *maitre d'*s of Paris. Bernard Sobelman, *Maître d'hôtel, la carte! Antoine Ventura maître d'hôtel* (Paris: Olivier Orban, 1987), 146.
28. Stephen Mennell, *Français et Anglais à table du Moyen Age à nos jours* (Paris: Payot, 1987), 65. Jean-Louis Flandrin, "Internationalisme, nationalisme et régionalisme dans la cuisine des XIVe et XVe siècles: le témoignage des livres de cuisine," in *Manger et boire au Moyen Age* (Nice: Publications de la faculté des lettres et des sciences humaines), 28:1 and (Paris: Les Belles Let-

tres, 1984), II:75–91. For his part, Jean-Louis Flandrin believes in a greater regional diversity insofar as working-class food is concerned. His study, which is based upon cookbooks, themselves codifying aristocratic and bourgeois cooking, makes evident a very great cosmopolitanism.

29. Pitte, *Histoire du paysage français*, I:115.
30. A. Maurizio, *Histoire de l'alimentation végétale depuis la Préhistoire jusqu'à nos jours* (Paris: Payot, 1932).
31. Louis Stouff, *Ravitaillement et alimentation en Provence aux XIVe et XVe siècles* (Paris-La Haye: Mouton, 1970), 106 and 243. Jacques Barrau, "Plantes vivrières et patrimoine culinaire: une réflexion sur le cas provençal," *Information sur les sciences sociales (SAGE)* 6 (1981): 925–946.
32. Stouff, *Ravitaillement et alimentation en Provence*, 261. Commented on by Barrau, "Plantes vivrières et petrimoine culinaire," 939.
33. Jean-Louis Flandrin, "Internationalisme, nationalisme et régionalisme," and "Problèmes, sources et méthodes d'une histoire des practiques et des goûts régionaux avant le XIXe siècle," in Jean Peltre and Claude Thouvenot, eds., *Alimentation et régions* (Nancy: Presses universitaires de Nancy, 1989), 347–361. Also see Platine (pseudonym of Jean-Louis Flandrin), "Variations franco-britanniques," *L'Histoire* 5 (October 1978): 102–103. Carole Lambert, "La cuisine française au bas Moyen Age: pays d'oïl et pays d'oc," in Peltre and Thouvenot, eds., *Alimentation et régions*, 375–385.
34. Anthelme Brillat-Savarin, *Physiologie du goût* (1965; new edition, Paris: Julliard, 1985), 261.
35. Arnold Van Gennep, *Manuel de folklore français contemporain* (Paris: Picard, 1946), I, II:501–541.
36. Ibid., 505–506.
37. Pierre Jourda, *Le Gargantua de Rabelais* (Paris: Nizet, 1988), 72–73.
38. Mikhail Bakhtine, *L'Oeuvre de Rabelais et la culture populaire au Moyen Age et sous la Renaissance* (Paris: Gallimard, "Tel" collection, 1988), 297.
39. Ibid., 280.
40. Enjalbert, *Histoire de la vigne et du vin*, 46.

2. Is Gourmandism a Sin in France?

1. Luke 22:34.
2. Matthew 11:18–19, Luke 7:33–35.

3. Jean-Paul Roux, *Jésus* (Paris: Fayard, 1990), 254.
4. Paul, Hebrews 4:15.
5. Paul, 1 Corinthians 6:13. We can read again in 1 Corinthians 6:19: "Shun fornication! Every other sin a man commits is outside the body; but the man who fornicates sins against his own body."
6. Jean Delumeau, *Le Péché et la peur. La culpabilisation en Occident, XIIIe–XVIIIe siècle* (Paris: Fayard, 1983).
7. Epictetus, *Manuel*, extracts translated by R. Létoquart (Paris: Hatier, 1964), 31–34.
8. *Règle de saint Benoît*, trans. Father Prosper Béranger (Tours: Mame, 1957), 30.
9. Ibid., 67–69.
10. Roger Dion, *Histoire de la vigne et du vin en France des origines au XIXe siècle* (Paris: Self-published, 1959).
11. Maurice Lelong, *Le Pain, le vin et le fromage* (Les Hautes-Plaines-de-Mane: Robert Morel, 1972), 11–48.
12. Ibid., 20–21.
13. Ibid., 28, 29, and 39. This text is similar to Saint-Sulpice's visit with the Bernardines, related by Anthelme Brillat-Savarin, *Physiologie de goût* (1965; new edition, Paris: Julliard, 1985), 392–398.
14. Rolande Gadille, *Le Vignoble de la Côte bourguignonne. Fondements physiques et humains d'une viticulture de haute qualité* (Paris: Les Belles Lettres, 1967). The Bordeaux geographers specializing in the history of wine, Henri Enjalbert and René Pijassou, maintain for their part that the premier *grand crus* of history appeared in Médoc in the seventeenth and eighteenth centuries. On the contrary, they date back to antiquity for André Tchernia, *Le Vin de l'Italie romaine* (Rome: Ecole française de Rome, 1986).
15. E. Charbonnier, "Manger et boire dans l'Ysengrinus," in Jean-Louis Flandrin, *Manger et boire au Moyen Age* (Nice: Publications de la faculté des lettres et des sciences humaines), 28:1 and (Paris: Les Belles Lettres, 1984), 410.
16. Quoted by Delumeau, *Le Péché et la peur*, 232. This example is English but representative of the entire West, because in the fourteenth century, the ways of eating and drinking well hardly differed in France and England, as Stephen Mennell has shown in *Français et Anglais à table du Moyen Age à nos jours* (Paris: Flammarion, 1987).

17. Quoted in Delumeau, *Le Péché et la peur*, 234.
18. Michel Rouche, “Les repas de fête à l’époque carolingienne,” in Flandrin, *Manger et boire au Moyen Age*, I:265–296.
19. Ibid.
20. Charbonnier, “Manger et boire dans l’Ysengrinus.”
21. Fernand Niel, *Albigeois et Cathares* (Paris: PUF, 1983).
22. Jean Duvernoy, “La nourriture en Languedoc à l’époque cathare,” *Carcassonne et sa région*, Acts of the 41st and 44th Conferences of Regional Studies held by the Historic Federation of Mediterranean Languedoc and Roussillon (Carcassonne, 1970), 235–241.
23. Emmanual Todd, *L’Invention de l’Europe* (Paris: Le Seuil, 1990).
24. Ibid., 110.
25. Niel, *Albigeois et Cathares*, 67–68.
26. Denis de Rougemont, *L’Amour et l’Occident* (Paris: Plon, 1939 and “10–18” collection), 1962.
27. R. Lassalle, “Le dit et le non-dit culinaires dans la littérature narrative de langue d’oc,” in Flandrin, *Manger et boire au Moyen Age*, I:441–447.
28. *Propos de table de Martin LUTHER* (Paris: Borneo, n.d.), I:100–101.
29. Ibid., 133.
30. Ibid., 45.
31. This truly classic idea of Weber is hardly debatable. See Philippe Besnard, *Protestantisme et capitalisme* (Paris: Armand Colin, “U2” collection, 1970), 78.
32. Ibid., 79.
33. Ibid., 83.
34. *Le Figaro*, February 5, 1990.
35. Quoted in Jacqueline Boucher, “L’alimentation en milieu de cour sous les derniers Valois,” in J.-C. Margolin and R. Sauzet, eds., *Practiques et discours alimentaires à la Renaissance* (Paris: Maisonneuve et Larose, 1982), 161–176; see 163.
36. L. Vitet, *La Mort de Henri III* (Paris: H. Fournier, 1829), 85. I owe this reference to Xavier de Planhol.
37. Edmund Leites, *La Passion du bonheur. Conscience puritaine et sexualité moderne* (Paris: Le Cerf, 1988).
38. Ibid., 23, 39.
39. Voltaire, *Lettres philosophiques*, VI; quoted in ibid., 16.
40. Mennell, *Français et Anglais à table*, 158.

41. Onfray, *Le Ventre des philosophes*, 59.
42. Quoted in ibid., 66.
43. Ibid., 69. Also see Barbara Ketcham Wheaton, *L'Office et la bouche* (Paris: Calmann-Lévy, 1984), 274–279.
44. Quoted in Jean-Claude Bonnet, "Le système de la cuisine et du repas chez Rousseau," appendix to Serge Thériault, *Jean-Jacques Rousseau et la médicine naturelle* (Montreal: L'Aurore, 1979), 117–150; see 118.
45. Quoted in Onfray, *Le Ventre des philosophes*, 62.
46. Bertin, Lettre à Mme de Parn, in *Oeuvres complètes* (Paris, 1824), 325. I owe this reference to Xavier de Planhol.
47. Hélène Sarrazin, *Elisée Reclus ou la passion du monde* (Paris: La Découverte, 1985), 21.
48. Louis Devance, "Stratégies de l'antialcoolisme en France au début du XIXe siècle," *Les Boissons: production et consommation aux XIXe and XXe siècles*, Acts of the 106th National Conference of Learned Societies (Perpignan, 1981; Paris: CTSH, 1984), 197–211.
49. The American Prohibition could only have come about in a predominantly Protestant country, and its violation by an Italian mafia could only have originated with citizens from a Catholic and Latin culture.
50. Karen Blixen, *Le Dîner de Babette* (Paris: Gallimard, 1988), 27–75.
51. Onfray, *Le Ventre des philosophes*, 179–200.
52. See, for example, her interview with Jacques Nerson, *Le Figaro-Magazine*, July 16, 1988.
53. *Le Figaro*, December 21, 1983.
54. *Le Figaro*, July 4, 1990.
55. Todd, *L'Invention de l'Europe*.
56. *Catéchisme du Saint Concile de Trente*, trans. Emmanuel Marbeau (Paris: Desclée, 1936), 532.
57. Louis de Grenade, *Le Guide des pécheurs*, retranslated by the R.P. Cyprien de Sainte-Angélique (Lyon, 1674), 646. Quoted by Marcel Israël, preface to Balde, *Urania Victrix*, selected texts translated and annotated by Andrée Thill, University of Haute-Alsace, Center for Rhenish Research and Studies (Mulhouse, 1989), xi. I owe the reading of Jacob Balde to Gabriel Wackermann.
58. Sainte Theresa of Avila, *Le Château de l'âme*, quoted in ibid., xix.
59. Gillet, *Par mets et par vins*, 130–131.
60. Quoted in Israël, preface to Balde, *Urania Victrix*, xix.

61. Michel Serres, *Les Cinq Sens* (Paris: Grasset, 1985).
62. Balde, *Urania Victrix*, 42.
63. *Vie de Pascal*, by Mme Périer, his sister, in Pascal, *Pensées* (Paris: Garnier, 1964), 35.
64. Ibid., pensée 71:86.
65. *Sois bon soldat*, by a veteran of the French army (Lille et Tunhout: Universal Catholic Printing Office, 1913), 27 and 123. I owe this reference to Colette Fontanel.
66. Canon François Turcq, *A toi, jeune homme, ce "code de la route"* (Paris: SPES, 1942), 29. I owe this reference to Colette Fontanel.
67. Robert Sauzet, "Discours cléricaux sur la nourriture," in Margolin and Sauzet, eds., *Practiques et discours*, 247–252.
68. Names are withheld here so as not to endanger their fair consideration in Rome, which thinks these things but does not express them in words.
69. Delumeau, *Le Péché et la peur*, 477.
70. Quoted in Sauzet, "Discours cléricaux sur la nourriture," 250.
71. *Introduction à la vie dévote*, 1609, chap. 39; quoted in ibid., 251.
72. Brillat-Savarin, *Physiologie du goût*, 172.
73. Dom Paul Delatte, *Commentaire de la règle de saint Benoît* (1919; new edition, Sablé: Saint-Pierre de Solesmes Abbey, 1969), 261–267.
74. Most are published by Robert Morel.
75. Serge Bonnet, "Auricoste de Lazarque est-il au ciel?," preface to Auricoste de Lazarque, *La Cuisine messine* (Nancy: Presses universitaires de Nancy and Editions Serpenoise, 1986), 5–8.
76. Migne, *Dictionnaire des passions, des vertus, des vices et des défauts. Encyclopédie théologique* (Paris, 1848), col. 509.
77. Bernard Alexandre, *Le Horsain* (Paris: Plon, 1988).
78. Ibid., 72.
79. V. Poucel, *Plaidoyer pour le corps* (Le Puy, 1944), 198 and 205. Quoted in Jean Hani, "Nourriture et spiritualité,"in Simone Vierne, ed., *L'Imaginaire des nourritures* (Grenoble: Presses universitaires de Grenoble, 1989), 137–149.

3. Governing at the Table: Birth of a Model

1. Louis XIII consumed a teaspoon of anise seed after each meal, to aid digestion. *Journal de Jean Héroard* (Paris: Fayard, 1989).

2. Noël du Fail, "La retraite d'Entragel," *Contes et discours d'Entragel* (ed. de Paris, 1875). Quoted by Pierre de Vaissière, *Gentilshommes campagnards de l'Ancienne France*, ed. Christian Bertillat (1903; reprint, Paris: Estrépilles, 1986).
3. Cited by Emma Rothschild, "Haute culture-haute cuisine ou Hangtcheou-sur-Seine," *Le Débat*, April 11, 1981, 125–132. I owe this reference to Pierre Nora.
4. Quoted by Henri Gault and Christian Millau, "Bibliothèque de Guides bleus," *Guide gourmand de la France* (Paris: Hachette, 1970), 336. Stefan Zweig (*Erasme* [1935; reprint, Paris: Grasset, 1988], 70–71) describes Erasmus's passion for eating well in this way: "Each day he needed to drink Burgundy wine to accelerate the circulation of sluggish blood. . . . He passionately loved well-prepared dishes; as a faithful disciple of Epicurus, he had an inexpressible fear of bad food. . . . The subtlety of his senses induced lethargy in him, and refinement became a true necessity."
5. Joseph Berchoux, *La Gastronomie ou l'homme des champs à table. Poème didactique en IV chants pour servir de suite à l'Homme des Champs* (1801; reprint, Grenoble: Glénat, 1989), 44.
6. Anthelme Brillat-Savarin, *Physiologie du goût* (1825; reprint, Paris: Julliard, 1965), 354.
7. Paul de Courselles and Sixte Delorme, *En route avec l'oncle Mistral* (Paris: Librairie Ducrocq, 1900), 44–45.
8. Jean-Robert Pitte, "Une lecture ordonnée de la carte des fromages traditionnels de France," in Pierre Brunet, ed., *Histoire et géographie des fromages* (Caen: Center for Studies on the Evolution of Rural Life, 1987), 201–207.
9. Claude Thouvenot, *Le Pain d'autrefois* (Paris: André Leson, 1977), 67.
10. Robert Courtine, *Balzac à table* (Paris: Robert Laffont, 1976), 67.
11. Information provided by Gérard Sivéry.
12. The idea of applying Von Thünen's theory to the geography of cheeses comes from Françoise Clavel.
13. Albert Rigaudière, "La Haute-Auvergne face à l'agriculture nouvelle au XVIIIe siècle," in *Etudes d'histoire économique rurale au XVIIIe siècle* (Paris: PUF, 1965), 1–104; see 20, 61–62, 92–94.
14. Gruyère.
15. Guy Thuillier, "L'alimentation en Nivernais au XIXe siècle," in Jean-

Jacques Hemardinquer, ed., *Pour une histoire d'alimentation* (Paris: A. Colin), *Cahiers des Annales* 28 (1970): 153–173.

16. Emile Zola, *Le Ventre de Paris* (1873; reprint, Paris: Le Livre de Poche, 1978), 385–388. Emile Zola's famous text perfectly illustrates von Thünen's theory. The crescendo of odors and adjectives corresponds to the possibilities for conserving and transporting cheeses—that is, their degree of hardness—or to their distance from the Parisian market.
17. Auguste Escoffier, *Souvenirs inédits* (Marseilles: Jeanne Laffitte, 1985).
18. Ibid., 184–185.
19. François Villon, IX, 17, *Ballade des femmes de Paris*:

Princes, aux dames parisiennes
De beau parler donnez le prix;
Quoiqu'on die d'Italienne
Il n'est bon bec que de Paris.

(*Ballad of the Women of Paris*
Princes, to the Parisian ladies
For beautiful speech give the prize;
Although they speak of Italian
Only in Paris is there lovely chatter.)

Also see Jean-Robert Pitte, "Le rayonnement gastronomique de Paris," *Cahiers du CREPIF* 9 (1984): 211–219.

20. There is abundant literature on the two works just mentioned. There is commentary on them in Barbara Ketcham Wheaton, *L'Office et la bouche* (Paris: Calmann-Lévy, 1984); in Stephen Mennell, *Français et Anglais à table du Moyen Age à nos jours* (Paris: Payot, 1987); and in Jean-Louis Flandrin, ed., *Manger et boire au Moyen Age* (Nice: Publications de la faculté des lettres et des sciences humaines) and (Paris: Les Belles Lettres, 1984), particularly in volume II.
21. Jérôme Lippomano, "Relation Lippomano," in *Relations des ambassadeurs vénitiens sur les affaires de France au XVIe siècle*, collected by Tommaseo (Paris, 1838); quoted with commentary by Philippe Gillet, *Par mets et par vins. Voyages et gastronomie en Europe (XVIIe–XVIIIe siècles)* (Paris: Payot, 1985); Jean-François Revel, *Un festin en paroles* (Paris: Pauvert, 1979), 175–178. This testimony is confirmed by Thomas Platter in 1599; quoted by Gillet, *Par mets et par vins*, 58–59.

Jérôme Lippomano's opinion is again shared by Alfred Fabre-Luce in the middle of the twentieth century: "Food has unbalanced the average French budget. In 1939, the poor Parisian spends three times more for his food than he would need to subsist on" (*Journal de la France*, August 1940–April 1942 [Paris: Impr. JEP, 1942]; quoted by Gérard Miller, *Les Pousse-au-jouir du maréchal Pétain* [Paris: Seuil, 1975]).

22. Grimod de la Reynière, *Ecrits gastronomiques* (Paris: coll. "10–18," 1978), 229–231. Jean-Robert Pitte, "L'approvisionnement gastronomique de Paris au début de XIXe siècle," *L'Art culinaire au XIXe siècle. Antonin Carême* (Paris: Délégation à action artistique de la Ville de Paris, 1984), 47–53.
23. De la Reynière, *Ecrits gastronomiques*, 266.
24. Brillat-Savarin, *Physiologie du goût*, 308–309 and 313.
25. Ibid., 177.
26. Ibid., 152.
27. Eugène Briffault, *Paris à table* (Paris: Hetzel, 1846), 3–4.
28. Quoted by René Héron de Villefosse in the preface to Roger Lallemand, *La Cuisine de Paris and de l'Ile-de-France* (La Rochelle: Quartier Latin, 1975), 8–9.
29. Jean-Robert Pitte, *Histoire du paysage français* (Paris: Tallandier, 1986), II:14–40.
30. Mennell, *Français et Anglais à table*, 159.
31. G. Hyvernat-Pou, "Un repas princier à la fin du XVe siècle d'après le Roman de Jehan de Paris," in Flandrin, ed., *Manger et boire au Moyen Age*, I:261–264.
32. Zeev Gourarier, "Le 'banquet' médiéval (XIVe–XVIe siècle)," in *Les Français et la table* (Paris: Musée des ATP, 1985), 149–161; see 157.
33. Jacqueline Boucher, "L'alimentation en milieu de cour sour les derniers Valois," in J.-C. Margolin and R. Sauzet, *Practiques et discours alimentaires à la Renaissance* (Paris: Maisonneuve et Larose, 1982), 161–176.
34. Alain Girard, "Du manuscrit à l'imprimé: le livre de cuisine en Europe aux XVe et XVIe siècles," in Margolin and Sauzet, *Practiques et discours*, 107–117; and various works by Maxine Rodinson quoted by A. Girard.
35. James Dauphine, "Bonvesin de la Riva, *De Quinquaginta curialitatibus ad mensum*," in Flandrin, ed., *Manger et boire au Moyen Age*, II:7–20.
36. Chantilly Museum.
37. Jean-François Solnon, *La Cour de France* (Paris: Fayard, 1987), 60–61.

38. Alain Gruber, *L'argenterie de maison du XVIe au XIXe siècle* (Fribourg: Office du Livre, 1982), 10, 122.
39. Boucher, "L'alimentation en milieu de cour sour les derniers Valois," 172.
40. Ibid., 171.
41. Ibid., 173.
42. Ibid.
43. *Journal de Jean Heroard* (Paris: Fayard, 1989).
44. Prosper Montagné, "La table et l'alcôve du 'Grand Roy': La Table," in John Grand-Carteret, *L'Histoire, la vie, les moeurs et la curiosité par l'image, le pamphlet et le document (1450–1900)*, 4 vols. (Paris: Librairie de la curiosité et des Beaux-Arts, 1928), III:375–385; see 375.
45. Ibid.
46. Ibid.
47. Jack Goody, *Cuisines, Cuisine and Classes* (Paris: Centre de création industrielle, Centre Georges Pompidou, 1984), 171. Jean-Louis Flandrin, Philip and Mary Hyman, "La cuisine dans la littérature de colportage," présentation de *Le Cuisinier françois* (Paris: Montalba, "Bibliothèque bleue," 1983), 11–99.
48. Ibid., 96.
49. Ibid., 18 sq.
50. *Le Cuisinier françois*, 192.
51. This was the characteristic that shocked the first Japanese who came to visit France in 1862. Here is an extract from a letter written May 9 to his superiors by Shibata Teitaro, an official for the Foreign Relations Service (quoted in *Le Japon et la France. Images d'une découverte* [Paris: Publications orientalistes de France, 1974], 52):

> We are troubled by the food, which is different. No matter where you go, you are served all the most prized dishes, most of which are based upon meat. If this meat is replaced with fish, it is cooked in oil. There is no variation in the vegetables and if, by chance, we are served some, they, too taste like fat. As this cooking with butter does not suit us, we fixed ourselves a kind of *sashimi* during our stay in France, by cutting up raw fish and sprinkling it with the sauce we brought along. Since the beginning of our mission abroad, that was the first time we found any food that satisfied us.

52. Quoted by Flandrin and Hyman, "La cuisine dans la littérature de colportage," 27.
53. Engraving reproduced in Revel, *Un festin en paroles*, 155.
54. Wheaton, *L'Office et la bouche*, 47–48.
55. In the Middle Ages, *potage* referred to all dishes prepared in a pot.
56. Molière, *L'Avare*, 1668, III:1.
57. Wheaton, *L'Office et la bouche*, 133 and 140.
58. Annick Pardailhé-Galabrun, *La Naissance de l'intime. 3000 foyers parisiens, XVIIe–XVIIIe siècles* (Paris: PUF, 1987).
59. Françoise Thinlot, *Maisons de Bourgogne* (Paris: Hachette, 1974), 99–100.
60. This is only in a manner of speaking, because on many roofs, tiles or slate began to replace thatch in this period.
61. Boucher, "L'alimentation en milieu de cour sour les derniers Valois," 172.
62. Isabelle Maillard, "L'art de la table au XVIIIe siècle," in *Les Français et la table*, 202–211; see 206.
63. Quoted by Wheaton, *L'Office et la bouche*, 174.
64. Mennell, *Français et Anglais à table*, 52.
65. Brillat-Savarin, *Physiologie du goût*, III:21. On this theme, see Wheaton, *L'Office et la bouche*, 165–185.
66. The eighteenth century was the century for women in high society. Paul Hazard (*La Pensée européenne au XVIIIe siècle* [1978; reprint, Paris: Fayard, 1990], 251) writes, "Balls, dinners, suppers, were moments in their great continuous holiday."
67. Jean-Robert Pitte, "Dom Pérignon à la lumière de l'histoire," *L'Amateur de champagne* 1 (May 1988): 11–16.
68. Quoted by Ernest Kahane, *Parmentier ou la dignité de la pomme de terre. Essai sur la famine* (Paris: Albert Blanchard, 1978), 72.
69. Jean-Robert Pitte, "Il était une fois le foie gras," *Le Point* 484 (December 28, 1981): 48–49.
70. Gault and Millau, *Guide gourmand de la France*, 133–138.
71. François Bonneau, *Talleyrand à table* (Valençay: Chez l'auteur, 1990), 84.
72. Gault and Millau, *Guide gourmand de la France*, 594–596.
73. Forty-five percent of the French list it among their favorite cheeses, which earns it first place. SOFRES poll published in *Cuisine et vins de*

France 400 (September 1984): 23. Camembert is so highly valued in the French imagination that a short story by Noëlle Châtelet ("Troc," *Histoires du bouches* [Paris: Mercure de France, 1986, "Folio," 1988], 100–107), presents a French jeweler who lives in Lima and who exchanges a gold signet ring for a Camembert cheese with a sailor from the *Jeanne d'Arc* put in at the port of Callao. Originally from Elbeuf, he has gone without it for ten years. . . .

74. Gault and Millau, *Guide gourmand de la France*, 640–641. The origins of the Camembert legend are discussed solemnly in Pierre Boisard, *Le Camembert, mythe national* (Paris: Calmann-Lévy, 1992).
75. Jean-Robert Pitte, "Gastronomie," in Jean Tulard, ed., *Dictionnaire Napoléon* (Paris: Fayard, 1987).
76. Bonneau, *Talleyrand à table*, 84.
77. Jean-Claude Bonnet, "Carême ou les derniers feux de la cuisine décorative," *Romantisme* 17–18 (1977): 23–43.
78. Jean Moura and Paul Louvet, *La Vie de Vatel* (Paris: Gallimard, 1929).
79. Bonneau, *Talleyrand à table*, 84.
80. Fanny Deschamps, *Croque-en-bouche* (Paris: Albin Michel, 1976), 24.
81. *Le Figaro-Magazine*, March 10, 1990, 182.
82. Ibid.
83. *Le Monde*, April 15, 1988, 8.
84. Theodore Zeldin, *Histoire des passions françaises* (Paris: éd. Recherches, "Encres," 1981), III:423.
85. Quoted by Edmond Neirinck and Jean-Pierre Poulain, *Histoire de la cuisine et des cuisiniers. Techniques culinaires et practiques de table en France du Moyen Age à nos jours* (Paris: Fernand Lanore, 1988), 29.
86. Quoted by Wheaton, *L'Office et la bouche*, 202.
87. Ibid., 203. Guy Penaud, "Monsieur Noël, le Périgourdin qui travaillait pour le roi de Prusse," *Périgord-Magazine* 37 (1983): 34–35.
88. Wheaton, *L'Office et la bouche*, 205–209.
89. Philippe Mordacq,*Le Menu. Histoire illustrée* (Paris: Robert Laffont, 1989).
90. Mennell, *Français et Anglais à table*, 168.
91. *Le Point* 898 (December 4, 1989).
92. Hisahide Sugimori, *Tenno no ryoriban* (Tokyo: Shueisha, 1982).
93. Maillard, "L'art de la table au XVIIIe siècle."
94. *La Table d'un roi. L'orfèverie du XVIIIe siècle à la cour de Danemark* (Paris: Musée des Arts décoratifs, 1987).

4. The Gastronomic Restaurant, *or* Haute Cuisine *on the Streets*

1. Stephen Mennell, *Français et Anglais à table du Moyen Age à nos jours* (Paris: Payot, 1987), 197–208. Philippe Gillet, *1989 est également l'année du bicentenaire du restaurant* (Paris: Chambre syndicale de la haute cuisine française, 1989); Valérie Ortoli, *Paris, capitale de la gastronomie. 200 ans de restauration* (Paris: Direction générale de l'information et des relations extérieures de la mairie de Paris, 1984).
2. Mennell, *Français et Anglais à table*, 197–200.
3. Henri Enjalbert, *Histoire de la vigne et du vin. L'avènement de la qualité* (Paris: Bordas, 1976), 199.
4. Ibid., 199.
5. Cited by Edmond Neirinck and Jean-Pierre Poulain, *Histoire de la cuisine et des cuisiniers. Techniques culinaires et practiques de table en France du Moyen Age à nos jours* (Paris: Fernand Lanore, 1988), 49.
6. Anthelme Brillat-Savarin, *Physiologie du goût* (1825; reprint, Paris: Julliard, 1965), 306.
7. Fanny Deschamps, *Croque-en-bouche* (Paris: Albin Michel, 1976), 40–46.
8. Mennell, *Français et Anglais à table*, 202.
9. Sébastien Mercier, *Nouveau Tableau de Paris* (Paris, 1798); quoted by Valérie Ortoli, *Répartition des restaurants parisiens et aménagement urbain de la capitale*, master's thesis, Université de Paris-Sorbonne, 1986, 13.
10. Quoted by Neirinck and Poulain, *Histoire de la cuisine et des cuisiniers*, 55.
11. Theodore Zeldin, *Histoire des passions françaises* (Paris: éd. Recherches, "Encres," 1981), III:439.
12. Eugène Briffault, *Paris à table* (Paris: Hetzel, 1846), 154.
13. Neirinck and Poulain, *Histoire de la cuisine et des cuisiniers*, 74.
14. *Lyon, capitale mondiale de la gastronomie* (Lyon: éd. Lugdunum, 1935).
15. Grimod de la Reynière, *Lettre d'un voyageur à son ami ou réflexions philosophiques sur la ville de Marseille* (Paris: Plasma, 1979), 39.
16. Jean-Paul Aron, *Le Mangeur du XIX*e *siècle* (Lausanne: Ex Libris, 1974).
17. Robert Courtine, *Balzac à table* (Paris: Robert Laffont, 1976), 17–20.
18. The wood paneling of the Grand Seize salon, a few pieces of crockery, and some venerable old bottles are preserved today at La Tour d'Argent by Claude Terrail.

19. Maurice Guillemot, *Dîners parisiens* (Paris, 1901); quoted by Ortoli, *Répartition des restaurants*, 53.
20. Quoted in ibid., 54.
21. Mennell, *Français et Anglais à table*, 223.
22. Auguste Escoffier, *Souvenirs inédits* (Marseilles: Jeanne Laffitte, 1985), 192–193.
23. See above the passage on green asparagus from Villelaure.
24. Neirinck and Poulain, *Histoire de la cuisine et des cuisiniers* 93. On Escoffier and his international influence, also see Mennell, *Français et Anglais à table*, 226–239.
25. Deschamps, *Croque-en-bouche*, 194–195.
26. Paul Gerbod, "La restauration ferroviaire d'hier et d'aujourd'hui," in Alain Huetz de Lemps and Jean-Robert Pitte, eds., *Les Restaurants dans le monde et à travers les âges* (Grenoble: Glénat, 1990), 417–425.
27. Ibid.
28. Pierre Benoît, *Le Déjeuner de Sousceyrac* (Paris: Albin Michel, 1931).
29. Marcal Pagnol, *Cigalon* (Paris: Presses Pocket, 1978), 13.
30. Maurice Lelong, *Le Pain, le vin et le fromage* (Les Hautes-Plaines-de-Mane: Robert Morel, 1972), 129–130.
31. Erckmann-Chatrian, *L'Ami Fritz* (Paris: Hachette, Le Livre de Poche, 1977).
32. Paul de Courselles and Sixte Delorme, *En route avec l'oncle Mistral* (Paris: Librairie Ducrocq, 1900).
33. Marcel Rouff, *La Vie et la passion de Dodin-Bouffant* (1924; reprint, Paris: Stock, 1970).
34. Quoted by Gaston Derys, *L'Art d'être gourmand* (Paris: Albin Michel, 1929), 18.
35. Simon Arbellot, *Curnonsky, prince des gastronomes* (Paris: Les Productions de Paris, 1965).
36. Jean-Yves Nau, "La superbe erreur des demoiselles Tatin," *Le Monde*, May 28, 1983.
37. Ortoli, *Répartition des restaurants*; Frédéric Moret, "Image et réalité de la restauration parisienne à travers les guides touristiques," in Huetz de Lemps and Pitte, eds., *Les Restaurants dans le monde et à travers les âges*, 27–30.
38. Brillat-Savarin, *Physiologie du goût*, XI:159.
39. In Roger Lallemand, *La Cuisine de Paris and de l'Ile-de-France* (La Rochelle: Quartier Latin, 1975), 128.

40. In Jacques Renoux, "Y a-t-il une gastronomie parisienne?" *Télérama*, February 3, 1982.
41. *Gault-Millau*, "Spécial 20 ans. C'était en 1969," supplement to issue LVI (December 1989).
42. Ibid., vi–vii.
43. Ibid., xii.
44. Jean-Paul Aron, *Les Modernes* (Paris: "Folio," 1986), 173.
45. *An 2000, A table* (Paris: Centre de création industrielle, centre Georges Pompidou, 1986), 49.
46. Aron, *Les Modernes*, 330.
47. Pierre-Marie Doutrelant, *La Bonne Cuisine et les autres* (Paris: Le Seuil, 1986), 23–30.
48. Paul Bocuse, *La Cuisine du marché* (Paris: Flammarion, 1976).
49. Grimod de La Reynière, "Sous la cloche, la cuisine charabia," *Le Monde*, May 24, 1986, 21.
50. Bernard Alexandre, *Le Horsain* (Paris: Plon, 1988), 352.
51. Claude Lévi-Strauss, *L'Origine des manières de table* (Paris: Plon, 1968), 411.
52. Lucette Chambard, "Mais dites-moi, où est donc la salle à manger?" *Cuisine et Culture. Les Amis de Sèvres* (June 2, 1984): 40–43.
53. Aron, *Les Modernes*.
54. Salvador Dali, *Dîners de Gala* (Paris: Draeger, 1967).
55. Jacques Renoux, "Y a-t-il une gastronomie parisienne?."
56. Ibid.
57. Michel Guérard, *La Grande Cuisine minceur* (Paris: Robert Laffont, 1976).
58. Among them, Jean-Claude Marcel, *La Sale Bouffe* (Paris: Bernard Barrault, 1990).
59. Alain Chapel, *La cuisine, c'est beaucoup plus que des recettes!* (Paris: Le Livre de Poche, 1987).
60. Rolande Bonnain-Moerdyk, "L'espace gastronomique," *L'espace géographique* 2 (1975): 113–126. Ortoli, *Répartition des restaurants*. Fanny Berland, *Aspects geographiques du restaurant Troisgros à Roanne*, master's thesis, Université de Paris-Sorbonne, 1988. François Blanchon, *Etude géographique des restaurants gastronomique de Paris*, DEA thesis, Université de Paris-Sorbonne, 1988. Guy Chemla, "L'évolution récente des restaurants gastronomique parisiens," in Huetz de Lemps

and Pitte, eds., *Les Restaurants dans le monde et à travers les âges*, 39–58.

Epilogue: Foods That Have a Soul: A Map of the Future for France

1. Bernard Sobelman, *Maître d'hôtel, la carte! Antoine Ventura maître d'hôtel* (Paris: Olivier Orban, 1987), 140.
2. Interview with Jean-Robert Pitte, *Gault-Millau*, October 1989, 45–46.
3. Ibid., 46–47.
4. Jean-Robert Pitte, "Français êtes-vous gourmets?," *Gault-Millau* 245 (October 1989): 33–42.
5. Jean-Claude Marcel, *La Sale Bouffe* (Paris: Bernard Barrault, 1990).
6. Ibid., 133.
7. Quoted by Jean-François Revel, *Un festin en paroles* (Paris: Pauvert, 1979), 271.
8. Matty Chiva, "Les enfants et la nourriture," *Le Monde de l'Education* (February 1979):8–10. *Le Doux et l'amer* (Paris: PUF, 1985).
9. Jacques Puisais and Catherine Pierre, *Le Goût et l'enfant* (Paris: Flammarion, 1987), 10–11.
10. Jacques Puisais, *Le Goût aujourd'hui* (Paris: Restaurateurs de métier des provinces françaises, n.d.) and *Le Goût juste des vins et des plats* (Paris: Flammarion, 1985). Emile Paynaud, *Le Goût du vin* (Paris: Dunod, 1980).
11. Jean-Marie Bourre, *La Diététique du cerveau* (Paris: Odile Jacob, 1990).
12. Institut français du goût, Centre culturel Mame, 19, rue Emile-Zola, 37000 Tours.
13. *Bibliothèque générale des écrivains de l'ordre de saint Benoît*, 1777–78, quoted by Roger Dion, *Histoire de la vigne et du vin en France des origines au XIXe siècle* (Paris: Chez l'auteur, 1959), 639.
14. Sobelman, *Maître d'hôtel*, 57–58.
15. Alain Chapel, *La cuisine, c'est beaucoup plus que des recettes!* (Paris: Le Livre de Poche, 1987), 55.
16. *Gault-Millau*, July 1977.
17. Glyn Daniel, *The Hungry Archeologist in France* (London: Faber and Faber, 1963).

18. Henri Desbois, *Le Charolais a-t-il un avenir?*, master's thesis, Université de Paris-Sorbonne, 1990.
19. Sylvain Zegel, "L'art de faire son beurre dans l'excellence," *Le Figaro*, March 19, 1990.
20. *Le Monde*. This law is the result of the Gilbert Jolivet report, *Rapport sur les appellations d'origine des produits autres que vinicoles* (Paris: Ministère de l'Agriculture, September 1989).
21. *Le Bien public*, October 31–November 1, 1989.

INDEX

The text of this book was set in 11.5/15 Fournier, licensed from Monotype/Adobe, a facsimile of a typeface designed by Pierre Simon Fournier le Jeune (1712–1768) in the 1740s. The face was originally called St. Augustin Ordinaire in the *Manuel typographique*, in which it first appeared. The structure of its letterforms is inspired by the Romain du Roi of 1702 by Philippe Grandjean (1666–1714), a transitional face between the historical periods of neoclassicism and rococo. The present-day version of Fournier was first introduced by the Monotype Corporation in 1924 as Monotype Fournier. Rational and yet exquisitely florid, it is a typeface of clean look and even color.

This book was designed by Linda Secondari.
Spot illustrations by Martha Lewis.
Composed by Audrey Smith.
Printed and bound at Thomson-Shore.

STONEHAM PUBLIC LIBRARY
3 1509 00555 8419

DATE DUE

STONEHAM
APR 22 2002
PUBLIC LIBRARY